Advance Praise for *Fix Your Business*

"Melinda Emerson has developed a detailed process that when followed, will positively impact your business. She will help you find time to read this book and implement its teachings using her "12 Ps of Running a Successful Business."

W. Kenneth Yancey, Jr.,
CEO, SCORE

"Fix Your Business gives you a step-by-step way to get yourself back in charge. It's an organized, practical makeover for your business, written by a world-class expert, known and respected by millions of business owners."

Tim Berry
Author, *Lean Business Planning*

"If you want a roadmap for business success you must read Fix Your Business by Melinda Emerson. Her 12 Ps of Running a Successful Business lay the groundwork to build a scalable business that will allow you to live your dream life."

Jon Gordon
Bestselling Author, *The Power of Positive Leadership*

"Melinda Emerson has written a fabulously practical guide to help small businesses scale and address the many challenges that exist on that journey. I love her 12 Ps which, frankly, businesses of any size could learn from. And the short fixes are genius. This is a must-read for anyone owning their own business."

Sharon Rowlands
CEO, ReachLocal

FIX YOUR BUSINESS

BY:
MELINDA F. EMERSON

FIX YOUR BUSINESS

A 90-Day Plan to Get Back Your Life and Remove Chaos From Your Business

BY:
MELINDA F. EMERSON

Authority Publishing
Gold River, California

FIX YOUR BUSINESS: A 90-Day Plan to Get Back Your Life and Remove Chaos From Your Business

By Melinda F. Emerson

1. BUS020000   2. BUS025000   3. BUS060000

Published by Authority Publishing, Gold River, California
www.succeedasyourownboss.com

First Edition

ISBN: 978-1-935953-88-3
Ebook: 978-1-935953-89-0

Printed in the United States of America

10 9 8 7 6 5 4 3

Authority Publishing
11230 Gold Express Dr. #310-413
Gold River, CA 95670
800-877-1097
AuthorityPublishing.com

DEDICATION

The book is dedicated to my amazing son, JoJo. I can't wait to see what you grow up to be. I love you to the moon and back.

TABLE OF CONTENTS

INTRODUCTION

Why your business needs this book

You've made it past the hard part. You've survived a few years, maybe more, in business, but your business is stressing you out. Why? Because you've built a business that can't run without you. It affects your sleep and your health. You are making some money and paying the bills, including your own paycheck (hopefully), but you dread dealing with your business at times.

Are you scared to take a vacation or any real time off? Your company cannot operate three days, let alone three months, without you. You are still the primary rainmaker in your business. You don't have sales staff or you have the wrong people working for you. No one thinks about how your business makes money other than you. Let's face it, if something happened to you, your business would probably cease to exist.

We all know payroll comes every two weeks whether your customers pay you or not. I've been there, and I wrote this book to help you Fix Your Business. I want you to have a business that allows you to love your dream life. I want you to develop processes and systems to get better control of your business. You might think that signs of failure are the ones you need to look out for when running your small business, but you need to pay just as much attention to evidence that your business is growing—before it grows so fast that you can't keep up with demand, and ultimately grow yourself out of business.

I've heard stories about businesses that got the attention of *Oprah Magazine* or business owners whose websites shut down just before the holidays because they were mentioned on *The Today Show* and couldn't keep up with orders. Or worse, they couldn't take orders because their merchant account was shut down due to unexplained volume. Or even worse, they couldn't fill orders due to poor cash flow management and lack of inventory. While on the surface these are good problems, they can mean devastation for your business if you're not prepared.

On the other hand, your longevity indicates that you're a rising star in the business world, and this book can help you shift your business strategy and operations to allow you to manage growth in a healthy way. I've designed it to help you fix your business in 90 days.

Regardless of the situation in your business, it can always be better. You started your business to make money. Your business should be working harder for you. With the right systems in place, this will happen.

After all, entrepreneurs live how most people won't, so we can live how most people can't.

After reading this book, you will be able to build a scalable business. You will know how to hire the right people to work for you, close more profitable deals, build a legacy for your family and employees, or position your business to sell someday if you wish. This book will give you the freedom to make that decision.

Please keep in touch, so I can continue to cheer you on.

Melinda Emerson
SmallBizLady

CHAPTER 1: PREPARATION
GET READY FOR REINVENTION

Does any of this describe your business?

- You are still doing too many jobs in your business.
- You feel like your business is running you.
- You fall into bed every night exhausted, knowing there's more work you could have done.
- Are you constantly stressing over cash flow issues?
- You've consistently made bad hires and have high employee turnover.
- You need to update your revenue model.
- You dread marketing.
- You know technology could help, but you don't know where to start.
- You have too many slow paying clients.
- You've become complacent.
- You do not have top-notch staff.
- You struggle with securing long-term contracts.
- You need more repeat business.
- You need to hire sales people.

Go ahead, check them off. This is your book; you're supposed to write in it.

As one business owner to another, if you don't have any of these problems, I doubt you would have picked up my book. And, if you have even a few, you're in the right place and you're in good hands.

I Can Hear You Now!

"Melinda, you can't fix my business in 90 days! That's just a come-on to sell books."

Okay, you're right. I can't fix your business at all. But I promise that the advice I'm offering will help you fix your business, and I've even designed it to help you fix your business in 90 days.

Here's the thing. Nobody's business is ever "fixed" as in "done," "perfect," or "nothing left to improve." Your business is always either a work in progress or you are out of business!

But in 90 days, you will

- review all the major functions of your business
- prepare action steps
- identify your biggest problems and know how you're going to resolve them
- solve some key issues
- have things under better control
- know where you're headed
- make a new Strategic Plan
- understand how to make planning a regular part of your business
- be able to *Fix Your Business* again, whenever you feel overwhelmed or you're ready to step up to another level of growth

After nearly 20 years in business, I have faced just about every problem that you are facing—some of them more than once.

Although I am proud to have a good education from Virginia

Tech, I sought out executive management, sales, and leadership training as my business grew. I did not learn how to run my business from MBA school. I learned it mostly by doing it and with the gracious help of my kitchen cabinet of advisors, mentors, and other business owners, and my own corporate clients who helped me grow as well.

So, let me tell you how this book works.

SmallBizLady's 12 Ps of Running a Successful Business

My "12 Ps" cover the most important areas of focus for your business. This book covers them one at a time in twelve chapters. Here is the list and an explanation of each P-word and how it's treated in the upcoming chapters.

	Chapter	*Subtitle*	*Contents*
1	**Preparation**	Get Ready for Reinvention	*How to use this book; your 90-day plan; options; growing too slowly; growing too fast; setting the stage; where and when to start.*
2	**Purpose**	Develop Your Leadership Mindset	*Grow yourself to grow your business; Why are you in business? What is your vision for the future? How are you going to channel the energy, passion, and courage to fix your business?*
3	**People**	Getting the Right Team and Advisors	*Developing your leadership style, formalizing your hiring process, employee onboarding, establishing a company culture, inspiring people to grow, managing people and personnel policies, gathering your kitchen cabinet of advisors.*

	Chapter	*Subtitle*	*Contents*
4	**Profit**	Managing Your Money	*Money management, cash flow, accounting, banking, credit, capital, going cashless, your collections process, pricing; and monitoring your profitability*
5	**Processes**	Build Systems to Delegate and Scale	*How to stop being the "Go-to" for everyone; preparing to delegate; creating workable systems and documenting procedures.*
6	**Productivity**	Use the Right Tools	*Invest in simplicity; how to make good technology decisions to save you time and money; how to make your business more productive and tech savvy.*
7	**Performance**	Measure Your Results	*What metrics do you need to measure in your business? Why and how customers buy from you: web traffic, lead generation, marketing efforts, open rates, conversion ratios, acquisition costs, shopping cart abandonment rates, and customer satisfaction.*
8	**Product**	Is Your Business Still Relevant?	*Know what you do best and who you do it for; What is your value proposition? Is your product still relevant? Is it time for a line extension or service innovation? And, are you still focused on the right niche?*
9	**Presence**	Building Your Brand Online and Offline	*Does your brand reflect who you are as a business now? Building brand presence, social media, online ads, content, promotion, and presentation; and mobile strategies and tactics.*

	Chapter	*Subtitle*	*Contents*
10	**Prospects**	Creating Your Sales System	*Who are you targeting? How are you reaching them? Creating your sales system; Hiring and managing a sales team; Does everyone sell?*
11	**Planning**	Update Your Strategy	*Plan and then plan some more, look at competitors and industry trends; from business plan to strategic plan to exit plan; employee stock ownership plan (ESOP) or Selling? What do you ultimately want?*
12	**Perseverance**	Being Strong Enough, Long Enough, To Win	*Staying ready for tomorrow's marketplace; anticipating customer needs; setting your planning cadence; taking your business to the next level.*

1. Your 90-Day Plan

90 days = 3 months = 12 weeks = 1 chapter per week

That's how we get to a 90-Day Plan. Ninety days equals about three months, which equals twelve weeks, plus a few extra days. That works out to one chapter per week, on average. But move ahead where you can to give yourself more time where you need it.

How much time will that take? Let's say you plan to allocate 30 minutes per day for this project. You can do it over lunch, or get up a half hour early or stay late or just squeeze it in. You have a chapter to read, some exercises to do, and some Fixes. Some are quick or easy, some are hard and require serious effort. Some are little changes in how you approach your everyday routine, but others require an investment of your money or your time or a change of your personal habits!

Your goal each week is to ***get it down*** so that whatever you are learning or deciding and figuring out can go into your plan.

Fix it now or put it in the plan to fix it when you can. Chapters 11 and 12 will help you put the longer-term pieces together.

2. Chapters

Each chapter covers one of my 12 Ps for Running a Successful Business. Within the chapter you'll find a discussion of the issue and a series of recommendations. You may find one chapter very elementary and feel that you have it completely under control. In another chapter, maybe you feel lacking in every topic I've covered. That's why I recommend that you use your time wisely—dig in deeper on some chapters and skim over others if you have those areas all set. Don't skip this chapter (1) or Chapters 11 and 12.

3. Expert Voices

Every chapter includes a candid interview that I conducted especially for this book with a small business expert on the topic of that chapter. Each expert also has a book, product, or online course of study that I am recommending to you to deepen your understanding of the business topic. You can find out more about the resources at FixYourBusiness.com.

4. Fixes

Throughout the chapters you'll find short fixes to do right away or to set aside for whenever you might need them. These fixes take five forms:

- Quick FIX – You can do this one fast.
- Personal FIX – Just for you, yourself.
- Team FIX – A fix for the team.
- Pre FIX – Do this one to keep yourself OUT of trouble.
- Mini FIX – This one's small but could be powerful.

Two pages of Topic-based Fixes come at the end of each chapter. These are ideas and actions that I may recommend or prompts to help you decide on steps to take during that week or to schedule for a future time. You'll come back to these in Chapter 11, when you do your Strategic Plan.

5. Emerson's Urgencies

When you reach the end of chapter work pages, you'll find a bold heading labeled **EMERSON'S URGENCIES**. That's me calling out directly to you.

"Do you have something going on that's tougher than a book is going to help you fix?"

We have all been there or we know someone who has, when the situation is URGENT.

- Your business lost your biggest customer.
- The bank is about to call your line of credit.
- You are about to lose your home.
- You are two years behind in payroll taxes.
- You are ill and afraid to tell anyone.

Watch for the Urgencies, and seek immediate help from your banker, lawyer, accountant, business coach, doctor, pastor, or another professional source.

6. Strategic Planning and Updating

Chapters 11 and 12 focus on various ways to implement best practices in business planning for the short term and longer term. When you have regular planning practices in place, you have fewer problems to stress you out, greater peace of mind, and a better quality of life as a business owner. You'll still need Fixes, but hopefully they won't be as severe or come as often as they do right now.

More Support

I have set up a private Fix Your Business Facebook group, and a website, FixYourBusiness.com, to provide extra support for you throughout this book and beyond. Online templates for the "Fixes" and all end-of-chapter worksheets are there, so you can download and fill them out on your laptop or tablet.

You will find additional references and resources for each chapter, links to all the resources I mention in the book plus many more, and opportunities for online courses and even a Mastermind Course with me. Links to books and online programs from all my featured experts will be there for you as well. My team will continue to add new resources to the website so we will grow with you.

Another Option

Well, there you have it. That's the **90-Day Turnaround Plan to Fix Your Business**. But I know you're an entrepreneur, and you have your own way of doing things, too, so I can offer an alternative in case it meets your needs better right now.

Deep Dive

Maybe you would rather cover these topics in more depth than one topic per week will allow. Maybe you really need to get your finances under control, and that would take a lot of time and work. Or maybe now's the time that you want to build the entire Human Resource function into your company. Perhaps you want to undertake a complete rebranding activity.
If that's the case, here's what I recommend.

- Take this first week to read Chapter 1 and carefully consider my 12 Ps of Running a Successful Business.
- If your business generally is in good shape, but there are a few areas where you really need to make some improvements, or

you have an opportunity to take your business to the next level, choose no more than three areas for deep focus.

- If your business is not in good shape, but you have a few areas that are about to take you under—cash flow management, for example, or not having any kind of a sales plan, or losing customers due to very poor customer service from your team, that could be another reason to choose three areas for a deeper focus, coming back to the other areas later.

To accomplish the Deep Dive, do this:

Week One:	Read Chapter 1 and select three Topics
Weeks 2 – 4:	Complete Chapter for Your Topic #1
Weeks 5 – 7:	Complete Chapter for Your Topic #2
Weeks 8 – 10:	Complete Chapter for Your Topic #3
Week 11:	Complete Chapter 11: Planning
Week 12:	Complete Chapter 12: Perseverance

Your Status Quo

What is the current state of your business? If it feels "just right," I'm going to worry you a little. It's really hard to just stay where you are for much time without any change or growth. The world will change around you too fast. That's why my book gets you paying attention to your Purpose, Product, and Presence in your chosen market space, as well as Planning and Perseverance. Just to make sure that you aren't missing something!

Henry Ford made the horse obsolete from the carriage; Elon Musk intends to make the driver obsolete from the car! Think of the goods and services that have become obsolete in your lifetime, plus the new things that have become commonplace. Innovation is the engine of entrepreneurship, and you are part of its fuel.

But maybe your business is really in trouble. It could be in trouble because you are in a negative growth situation, or you need to grow, but you're not sure how to go about it, or you're growing too fast and about to go off the rails! I'm here to help you in any scenario.

Are You Ready to Grow?

Lately, your business has felt like those too-tight skinny jeans at the back of your closet. You feel like you're going to bust at the seams, or that you might not be able to breathe if you start walking around. That's what your business feels like, too, when it isn't quite big enough to accommodate all the sales and expansion you're experiencing. Could this mean that it's time for a growth spurt? Here are some questions to consider to determine if you're really ready to grow your small business.

Do You Have Processes and Systems in Place?

Growth requires a heavy reliance on proven processes and systems. If you've been flying by the seat of your pants, making it up as you go along, you'll want to slow your roll and spend some time defining those processes.

Where do you need processes?

- In executing your marketing efforts
- In managing your billing and accounting
- In fulfillment and shipping
- In hiring and training staff

Essentially any task that is completed over and over again would benefit from a defined process. The idea is that once you grow and you're not the one executing every task, your employees can read through the list of instructions and complete the task without your assistance. You'll deal with this in Chapter 5, Processes.

How Much Money Does Growth Require?

Make no mistake about it: scaling your business will require funds. Whether you plan to hire additional staff to free you up to focus on strategy, you want to rent more office space, or you want to expand your product line, all of these require money. Build out a budget to understand what your growth costs will be, as well as any ongoing increases in your monthly overhead. Growing your business will grow your revenues, which will help cover these ongoing costs, but you still need an understanding of your upfront cash outlay to cover these expenses to see if you can even afford the step up. Consider these issues in the People, Profit, and Product chapters.

If you don't yet have the funds to support growth, and you don't want to take out a loan, make a plan to set aside a percentage of your monthly profit with a game plan for when you'll start to roll out your growth strategy. If you do decide to borrow money, a line of credit might be a good first step. Or maybe you have bigger capital needs. I'll discuss additional finance options in Chapter 4: Profit and Chapter 11: Planning.

How Much Additional Staff Do You Need to Hire?

Few entrepreneurs can grow their small businesses without adding employees or consultants to the team. Spend some time assessing what roles and responsibilities you will need a dedicated employee to handle so that you can focus solely on your company's growth. Payroll expenses tend to be among the biggest expenses in a business. If you can only afford to hire part-time help or contractors, plan to scale slowly until revenues increase enough to justify full-time staff. In this case the Profit and People chapters go hand in hand.

Will You Upsell to Your Existing Clients or Launch a New Product Line?

What does growth look like to your business? You essentially have two options: you can leverage your existing client base by working on upselling them additional products or services (a customer buys a dress, so you market a necklace and hand-bag to go with that dress), or you can launch an entirely new product line. The latter will require more energy and financial investment but could prove to be the more lucrative option. Do your research to decide which is the best strategy for long-term growth. These decisions come up in Chapter 8: Product, but you'll see them again in Chapter 9: Presence, Chapter 10: Prospects, and Chapter 11: Planning.

What Additional Technology or Equipment Will You Need?

Business growth often means you need more computers, tools, or technology, otherwise you'll struggle to meet demand as you rapidly scale. Get a plan for how you'll pay for anything you need to invest in, and then find the best resource and vendor for what you need to buy. Remember that leased equipment or used equipment is always an affordable option. Chapter 6: Productivity, is all about technology and tools, but your decisions will also impact your moves in Chapter 4: Profit and Chapter 11: Planning.

Do You Have the Mental Bandwidth That Growth Requires?

Beyond finding the money, hiring new employees, and creating a game plan for your business growth, you really want to make sure you're mentally and emotionally ready for such a big step in your business' development.

Likely, growing your business will require you to spend more time at work, which will impact your ability to spend time with your loved ones. And if you have any other major life events happening, such as getting married, moving, having a baby, or taking care of aging parents, you might not want to add such a large responsibility to your plate right now.

It's important that you understand exactly how much time commitment growing your business will demand, as well as how much brain space it will eat up. It's essentially like starting your business all over again: you will devote a ton of time to planning and executing the growth plan, until the dust settles and you can find some equilibrium once your new team members are in place.

But ultimately, growing your business is a great opportunity to grow yourself. You'll test your boundaries, learn more, and find new successes for your company.

I'll address your mental state and your work and home life challenges in Chapter 2: Purpose, and again in Chapter 12: Perseverance. Chapter 11: Planning, is all about setting priorities, too, so that you can keep your commitments to a reasonable period. Just remember, growing your business isn't a sprint; it's a marathon.

Signs Your Small Business Is Growing Too Fast

I know, business growth sounds like a good thing. And it is. However, growing a small business requires planning, and I've seen businesses grow too fast. Uncontrolled growth can lead to going out of business quickly, too. You could burn through cash, exhaust your resources, make risky hiring decisions, and still fail to meet customer demand, and, above all, damage your brand.

When I give small business advice, I focus on the idea of controlled growth. In other words, I want entrepreneurs like you to plan for future growth. While you certainly want to take advantage of good opportunities that come your way, it's best to grow your business on a schedule. All business is not good business. If you see these red flags, your business might be growing a little too fast.

You're Fielding Customer Complaints Left and Right

When growing a business, you have to put the customer first. If your customers call with constant complaints, you might have overextended your staff resources. In my experience, rapid growth usually means that important things fall through the cracks in customer service. You can't respond to customers in a timely fashion because you don't have the manpower and resources. I help with this in Chapter 7: Performance.

You Don't Know Where You're Going to Get Funding

It's great to take lots of orders, but if you don't have the cash or a line of credit to keep up with inventory, raw materials, or hire the staff required, you will have a significant challenge. It's best to borrow money before you need it, because loans don't typically turn fast. Borrowing money when you are desperate and panicked is a great way to end up with a predatory loan with daily interest payments automatically deducted from your account. I've seen many business owners go bankrupt due to borrowing the wrong kind of money. Alternative lending can be a solution, but you still need a good credit score, clean accounting records, and bank statements to fill out all the required forms to secure financing. And if your monthly financial statements are non-existent or incomprehensible, that's going to slow down your ability to get financing from anyone. You want your financial statements and sales forecasts to be up-to-date, correct, and realistic; when they're not, you'll run into problems. And that's a sign you're growing too fast.

Growing a small business takes time. You'll need to give yourself a chance to learn the ropes, adjust to changing customer needs, develop new marketing techniques, and figure out which vendors to use. Growing your business too fast may lead to unintended consequences. We'll cover these issues in Chapter 4: Profit, as well as in Chapter 2: Purpose and Chapter 11: Planning.

You're Making Decisions Quickly

When your business starts to take off, you'll need more employees, better training, inventory management software, logistics support, high volume shipping options, and you must get them all now.

The problem with this situation is that everything is urgent. You don't have the time to do much research to learn about options to make the best decisions. You don't comparison-shop for equipment, for example, or vet new hires thoroughly enough. You need well-defined processes and systems in place, so that you do not get pulled under by a huge order or your product becoming the hot Christmas toy. Long-term financial and operational decisions don't need to be made in a rush. If this is where you are in your business, just go through all the chapters and fix all the areas that need to be tightened up!

You Don't Know What Type of Growth You Want

Believe it or not, there are many ways to grow a business. For instance, if you sell consumable products, such as bath products or laundry detergent, you might want to focus on increasing repeat customers.

On the other hand, if your products are one-time buys, you might need to launch a new product line and develop a broader marketing campaign to increase market share.

If you don't know how you want to grow your business, you can't scale it responsibly. Don't wait until you get overwhelmed; slow down and start thinking through your growth strategy. Chapter 8: Product and Chapter 11: Planning offer keys to start working through this.

You're Stressed Out and Tired

All entrepreneurs have late nights or early mornings. Stress is part of running a small business, but it shouldn't be your constant companion. If chronic stress is keeping you up at night or affecting your health, then you need to make different choices about how your business runs or whether you should still run the business.

If you're stressed out most days at work, your business is

probably growing too fast. Or worse, your business isn't growing at all. If you are not emotionally in balance, with a plan to get things under control, you could start projecting those feelings onto your staff, customers, and your loved ones, which may derail future growth and your closest relationships.

Getting Started

Now you're almost ready to go! But I want you to take this seriously as a 90-day plan. Don't just pick it up and put it down when you have a free moment, because we both know you don't have "free moments." Make time to work on your business in your schedule, just as you would prioritize scheduling a customer meeting, otherwise you will not get it done. You owe that to yourself and to your business.

I'll give you a few options to think about. What works for you depends on the nature of your business, your family situation, whether you travel heavily, and your personal preferences. So, work out a plan that works for you, just like you do everything else. But do, please, build a plan.

1. Set aside 30 minutes per work day (M-F) at the same time every day.

2. Set aside a morning or afternoon, either on a workday or weekend day, to read the chapter and work on action steps.

3. Do the 90-Day Plan with a fellow business owner and become accountability partners for each other. Add a check-in meeting or phone call each week to keep yourselves on track.

4. Join my private Fix Your Business Facebook group for motivation and accountability. You'll get a chance to ask me questions during my live Q&A sessions.

5. Check out FixYourBusiness.com for additional resources.

Other Considerations

Pick a good time to do this. You need three months to get it done right. So, look for three relatively normal to slow months—not over the holidays, you need rest and to enjoy your family. If you have more of a week-on/week-off schedule with your children, look at your time that way.

Everyone's life is different; just try to be consistent. You also want to get out of the office or your home to do this work, you need to eliminate distraction and interruptions. When I was working on this book, I wrote from 5 a.m. to 7 a.m., three days a week. You can make the time to do this.

Getting the Work Done

Some "Fixes" are things I'm asking you to think about and write down. Others involve your team. Still others involve being with other people during business hours, or they require investments that you won't be ready to make right away.

I don't expect you to "finish" each chapter in one week. But I do expect you to read the entire chapter and work through all the questions and Action Steps at the end. Some of them you'll get done during the same week or within the 90 days. Some of them will be irrelevant to your business or will be things that you have totally under control! Congratulations—check them off and move on. Others will make their way into your Strategic Plan. But everything that *you* decide is important to you and your business will be recorded so that you can deal with it at the appropriate time.

Make your notes the fastest and easiest way for you. If you use a note taking tool like Evernote.com or OneNote, that's perfect. If you like to write in a journal, use my Fix Your Business 90-day planner. If you don't like to write or type notes, speak them into your smartphone or tablet; later you can send the audio files to temi.com or rev.com for inexpensive translation. Or use a voice-to-text tool if you have it. Just make it easy for yourself.

Now, let's get started!

FIX YOUR BUSINESS ACTION STEPS

Take these steps and add your own based on Chapter 1
PREPARATION

Which method have you chosen to Fix Your Business?	• 90-Day Plan • Deep Dive
If you've chosen Deep Dive, what 3 Ps have you selected?	1. 2. 3.
Of the 12 chapter topics, which are most problematic to you?	
Which topics are you most excited to work on?	
What issues do you want to remember from this chapter to help you later in planning?	
What is the Start Date of your 90-day Plan?	
What is the End Date when you will have completed Chapter 12?	
When will you set aside time on your schedule to get your plan completed?	

CHAPTER 2: PURPOSE
DEVELOP YOUR LEADERSHIP MINDSET

Your own mindset forms the core of your business. Your mindset drives your purpose and therefore it drives your business. Your purpose gives rise to your vision for your business. It's the manifestation of the long-term dream of what you want to accomplish as a business owner. And the way you behave as an owner, a manager, a boss, and colleague impacts your mindset about leadership.

Your mindset makes your business purposeful. It gives it a "why?" and explains the "what for?" Only you can inspire your business with purpose. And you should be clear on your own mindset about this purpose to inspire your team and your customers to take the journey with you.

Some people start their business with a purpose to help others. For example, there's Bombas (bombas.com):

Before launching Bombas, we learned that socks were the number one most requested clothing item at homeless shelters.

So, we started a company with the goal of solving that problem. For every pair of socks we sell, we donate a pair to someone in need. The more socks we sell, the more we can donate.

And to sell a lot of socks, we knew we had to design the best sock on the market.

The purpose of this company doesn't dictate the business model, but it suggests many of the ingredients. The founders wanted to solve a big problem: homeless shelters need a constant supply of socks for their residents. They could have started a not-for-profit venture to solve the sock problem. They could have started another kind of business, like manufacturing flashlights, and donated a portion of their profits to homeless shelters for socks. But they decided to marry their "doing good" purpose with their "doing well" purpose of building a successful business.

They could have made plain, warm serviceable socks for homeless people. But that choice wouldn't have built a huge, popular brand of unusual, outstanding socks, world-class socks that attract the attention of a huge audience of buyers who want to help and want to wear the socks themselves. And to invest in the homeless recipients of the socks with a gift of brand-new perfect designer socks that the giver is wearing, too, not just "warm socks" or "previously-worn" socks.

Their purpose drives a culture of love for their customers and unparalleled customer service and satisfaction. It's a virtuous circle of success.

You don't need to have a direct charitable purpose, and your business must make a profit or it will fail! Taking good care of yourself and your family is a noble purpose, as is educating your children, contributing to your community, creating new jobs, serving your customers, saving for your retirement, and becoming "the first one" to invent or accomplish or achieve something in business.

My own business purpose is "to end small business failure." A personal business challenge for me is to manage my scope, because my purpose can drive me to develop content and materials to coach and train small business owners, as well as to help big brands reach the small business market, or help big companies develop products and services to meet the needs of small businesses. If I were to go in too many directions at the same time without a strategy, I could get in big trouble. And like you, sometimes I have!

When you started out, you thought you had what it takes to be a successful entrepreneur. What do you think now?

There is a long list of the attributes of successful business owners, but my list is short, simple, and focused. Passion, Vision, and Flexibility. What's more, everyone has these qualities, just some of us have them in higher amounts than others.

Now's the time to have an honest conversation with yourself. Take note of these three characteristics to remind yourself what it takes to run a great business and why you do what you do.

1. Passion

When you have passion you're willing to bust through walls to get your message, tools, products, or services out to the world. That means: sticking to it when your family or life partner doesn't believe in you, or when your friends wonder when you'll get a "real job." Or when you lose your biggest customer and have to regroup. Passion is really about perseverance and working toward a future that can sometimes be uncertain. Your passion is the underlying element of your purpose, by doing the right things to serve your customers, and fixing your mistakes along the way, you'll watch your business grow! Focus on your passion whenever you're in doubt or feel overwhelmed. It is the core of "Why" you are in business.

2. Vision

You must have a big picture vision for your business. And you must have the ability to articulate your vision to your family, employees, funders, and customers. In some cases, you'll need to circle back to your original vision when times get a little tough. Your vision empowers you to see what your business can become. It allows you to anticipate the needs of your customers, before they appear. When you can predict the future in terms of what will come, what can be, and what your customer will need, that's how you stay ahead of the competition. To have this kind of vision takes guts. Doubt kills more businesses than anything else. You must trust yourself and commit to your vision to achieve it. You must believe that you are the one to provide your product or service. No matter how many others have tried it, your belief in your team's talents and yourself will make all the difference. You know the world needs your business. Your unique skills, service, products, and point of view will change the world. Executing your vision is about owning your true brilliance and channeling that to solve a problem for a specific niche customer.

Passion + Vision = Dreams turned into Reality.

3. Flexibility

When you see something isn't working, you must be 100% comfortable with changing direction and challenging conventional wisdom. You can find a way to make any situation work. Ignore suggestions that don't incorporate new ideas. Resist the tendency to react the way "you've always done it." Being a business owner is about making all the hard decisions, and often they have to be made quickly to save time, money, or a relationship. Never fall in love with your own idea or the sound of your own voice. It's about finding the best solution, no matter who makes the suggestion.

The quality of quick thinking and problem solving is a key leadership skill. This can be troublesome for people who over-analyze things, are stubborn, or may consider themselves introverted. But you must push forward even if you are apprehensive or didn't come up with the solution. You will feel fear. Everyone does. But your faith in yourself and your team must be bigger than your fear. At times you do need to slow down and focus on allowing great solutions to bubble to the surface. Business owners with the most flexibility and the best brainstorming with their teams tend to win.

Personal FIX
ENTREPRENEURSHIP QUALITIES

- Write down your top entrepreneurial qualities, each on a 3" × 5" card.
- Mine are Creative, Focused, Flexible. What are yours?
- On each card, jot a reminder to yourself about how you want to continue to develop that quality.
- Tape them to your bathroom mirror, your office door, on the wall just past your computer screen, or your closet door. Just remind yourself of who you really are. Even if you don't believe you have these traits now, you will develop them eventually.
- Read them out loud daily and start believing them now.

I am sure you do have the traits of a successful business owner. The key is to realize that you do and to let these characteristics run free within you, as this will translate into your business. Once that happens, stand back, look at your progress, and say "Wow. I made something happen."

Creating a Purpose-Driven Business

Now's the time to reconsider your purpose, to be sure that it still fits what you've become since you opened your doors and learned how things work in the business world. Maybe your purpose has changed, or maybe you've been too busy to really think about it. What you believe about "WHY" you are doing what you do is the backbone of your business.

Communicate your purpose to everyone in the company and through all channels to your customers. It's why you do the things you do, why people are hired, and why products and services are developed. Your purpose will challenge everyone to reach higher and do things they never dreamed they could achieve.

Once you've renewed your purpose, you need to articulate it as a big picture vision to your team and provide clarity and focus to where you are headed for the long run.

As a small business owner, you're automatically a leader, so not only must you have a vision, you must also be able to communicate it with everyone who you need to help you. You're constantly selling your vision to current and prospective employees, partners, investors, and advisors. It's important, because it's one thing to get things done, but motivation comes from remembering why you're doing it. What will the world be like when you achieve your purpose?

Keep in mind you may never achieve your big picture vision, but you will be achieving your purpose all the way. If I ever achieve my vision, all the people on earth who decide to start a small business will be successful, and there will be no more failures, ever. Right, it's not likely! But that's still my vision!

Consider the Bombas example. Maybe one day they will sell enough socks every day to meet the sock demand of all the homeless shelters in the world, and maybe other things will happen to reduce homelessness so that fewer socks are needed. I'll bet they will still be doing something in that business or another that involves helping people who need a helping hand. It's how they envision the world they want to live in.

On your journey as a small business leader, from idea to veteran entrepreneur, understanding your vision will help you do things better, keep your batteries charged, and inspire better work from your employees.

Real leaders rarely launch businesses only for recognition or money. They want to DO something! Putting visions into action is challenging, but outstanding leaders make it happen by setting demanding goals for their ventures and then pursuing them consistently. Inspired people who are committed to your vision helps tremendously too. You get people on board when you're able to articulate your vision. But you must also recognize that everyone in your life might not be able to see your vision. It takes persistence, and an incredible belief in yourself to walk the path to success. It may take unexpected detours, but being able to put your vision into words and pictures and having the strength to pursue it even when things are difficult are key characteristics of a successful business leader.

Here is an exercise for improving your visionary skills.

Mini FIX
VISION

- Identify a specific challenge within your business, such as solving a nagging problem with processing customer orders.
- Describe or draw out the "big picture" of how everyone benefits when that challenge is overcome.
- Make a list of ways to communicate your vision, including specific words and phrases.
- Rehearse your vision with an emphasis on what the situation will look like, feel like, and be like when the team has solved the problem.

Try this for a singular challenge where you can envision a solution, and then try it again for other challenges. Eventually articulating and expressing your vision, and inspiring your team to realize that vision, will become more natural to you.

Is Your Leadership Blocking Your Business Growth?

Most small business owners have thought about what kind of boss they want to be. Most of us have had terrible bosses, others of you have had perhaps one friendly, supportive boss whose style taught you something about how you wanted to run your own business. But whether friendly or aloof, outstanding bosses demonstrate leadership. They're not about using rewards and punishments to get things done, but about motivating, mentoring, and inspiring their team. These key leadership traits can work with just about any type of personality. So, what kind of boss are you becoming?

What Bad Bosses Do

Bad bosses "motivate" by intimidation or manipulation, and demand respect rather than earning it. Bad bosses micromanage. They don't trust their employees to be capable, so instead of delegating their desired outcome, they delegate only the task and then oversee it painfully, even destructively. Even good bosses may be guilty of doing this occasionally, but they recognize it and stop themselves (once someone brings it to their attention) before damaging morale.

Another breed of bad boss is the "know-it-all," who probably complains about employees and how they fall short. They never consider whether they set the employee up for failure with their poor leadership. Unrealistic bosses play the blame game, taking credit for things done well and blaming the team for all mistakes. Bad bosses are quick to anger and slow to praise.

What Good Bosses Do

Good bosses see themselves as a mentor to their team. When a mistake happens they first consider their role in it. What great bosses have in common is their level of support and recognition.

A good boss always has your back in a difficult situation with a customer or vendor. She is interested in you as a person and supports your career goals. She gives you credit for your good work rather than taking it herself.

People want to work for leaders who are interested in developing them, show trust, and show genuine interest in both the work and the employee's well-being. In other words, being a great boss isn't about having the right type of *personality*, but about practicing the right *leadership* day in and day out. We'll go much deeper into leadership styles in Chapter 3: People. Those leadership skills come from your leadership mindset—in other words, how you think about your purpose and your role in the company.

Caring Takes Many Forms

This is not to say that great bosses never use "tough love." While great bosses don't blow up at the slightest provocation, they aren't afraid to invoke disciplinary measures or have hard conversations when they are warranted. The best military leaders understand this, and they know how to instill a sense of putting the mission first, then the team, then the individual. If someone isn't pulling their weight, the truly caring boss finds out why and plans to address the problem.

Being a Great Boss Takes Practice

Outstanding bosses must have good ideas, confidence, and the ability to make on-the-spot decisions when necessary. They must also learn (often the hard way) how to rebound after a big mistake. All these characteristics require practice. It's like physical training: you become stronger by working those leadership "muscles" and learning from your mistakes. Sure, some people have more innate leadership capability than others, but even those blessed with good leadership skills must practice them to be the best possible leader.

Boosting Employee Engagement

Sometimes being a terrific boss requires stepping outside the normal routine. You and your team can become complacent. Occasionally it's beneficial to shake things up a bit. Do you hold regular staff meetings? When is the last time you did a retreat with the core team off-site? If you have a virtual team, when is the last time everyone saw each other face-to-face?

Team FIX
LEADERSHIP

- Host a non-work social activity, like a holiday lunch or bowling party. It doesn't have to be expensive; just plan ahead and make it thoughtful.
- Encourage employees to donate a certain number of hours per year to charity work. Even better, do some community service together.
- Celebrate achievements and milestones, even with hand-made in-house awards plus an afternoon off! Acknowledgment and appreciation of great work inspires more great work.
- Plan an occasional off-site retreat with a great facilitator for a wonderfully re-invigorating team experience to get everyone refocused.

Being a terrific boss is about being a leader. Great leaders are accessible, fair, and committed to the purpose. They have hard conversations in private. They consider multiple perspectives when making decisions. Some great leaders are teddy-bear friendly, while others are very formal. If you've been in the workforce long enough, you've encountered both types.

The best bosses elevate everyone around them. They aren't afraid to get into the trenches when the situation demands it, and they maintain conditions for everyone on the team to share ideas and concerns, shine, and demonstrate their unique brilliance. When the business starts to get into trouble, it's often best to look inward first.

Is your ego what's wrong with your business?

I must ask you this question because everyone close to you is afraid of it. Does your ego get in the way of your business leadership? Are you trying to hold all the information too close, trying to do it all yourself, afraid to let go of even the smallest decisions? I will get into how to let go in every chapter, but you've got to start with being honest. Fifty percent of all business problems are not-so-well-hidden personal problems, and if YOU are the biggest problem in your business, now is the time to fix it. Make changes now, before you run your business into the ground.

I understand how hard it is to be that honest with yourself. Depending on your answers to these questions, there may be an issue that you need to work on. There is a big difference between confidence and arrogance. And I can honestly give this advice because in my first few years in business, my relationships suffered because I built up a reputation as a young, talented, arrogant business owner. I lost business because there were people who just didn't want to deal with me. It's not enough to do good work, you must be good to work with and if your personality leans toward the arrogant side, you probably need a Fix.

Personal FIX
EGO CHECK

Answer these questions below honestly and review your approach.

- Are you a patient person?
- Do you always make decisions that are in the best interest of the business?
- Do you often seek advice or brainstorm with others?
- Do you ever share your personal shortcomings publicly with your staff?
- Do you tend to take business issues personally?
- Do you have trouble letting things go?
- Do you always need to get the last word?

> Make a list of a few key times that you made emotional decisions or had reactions that caused a business situation to get worse with a customer, vendor, or employee. Then, reflect on how you would handle things differently now.

Depending on how you answered the questions above, you now know some areas you need to work on. Ask three trusted people close to you if they think you come off as arrogant. Then work hard to consider your tone when you offer criticism and show more empathy for your team and others. You can say anything if you say it with love. Your personality will either draw people to you or repel people from you.

Finding Balance as a Business Owner

Finding an acceptable work/life balance might not happen until four or five years into your business. I just have to keep it real. I have found one of the best ways to deal with enjoying life more is by focusing on being present and being mindful of how people experience you. Multitasking is a great way to make a mistake or make someone important to you feel like you do not value them.

I remember when my son was in preschool. I had this habit of talking business on my cell phone when I picked him up from day care. I would often be on my phone the entire drive home after I put him in the car. Well, one day my son got in the car with me and said he wanted to talk to me. And I scolded him for interrupting me when I was on a business call. When we pulled into the driveway I got off the phone and turned and asked him what he wanted to talk about, and he said, "Nothing now, Mommy, I wanted to talk to you while we were driving home." Now that experience was quite a humbling and hurtful lesson, but I never did it again. Your family spells love: T-I-M-E! Don't be that parent at the ball game on your cell phone. Don't text or type while an employee is trying to talk to you. Focus on being present. Make eye contact when you speak and be a good listener. This will strengthen all your relationships.

Focus on Priorities

The real key to finding some semblance of balance is to set your priorities each day. As an entrepreneur, it is highly likely that you must spend far more of your waking hours working in your business than with your family or significant other. Start creating a Top 5 To-Do List every day. As you are wrapping up your day, write down a list of your top priorities for the next day. When you get to your office in the morning, start on those most valued tasks first and get them done before 11 a.m. Anything you accomplish after that is a bonus. Start with the task you consider most important or will take a significant amount of focus.

Common examples on setting priority lists include working on the thing closest to money first, taking on their hardest task first thing in the morning, or setting aside one day a week for specific tasks like content development. Some people can't start their day without a workout, yoga, or meditation. Some go right to making their daily sales calls, social media, facilitating a staff meeting, or proposal development. If you are still overworking, or too focused on your never-ending to-do list (which makes you feel like you haven't accomplished anything) then you need a Fix.

Mini FIX
DAILY PRIORITIES
MY TOP FIVE

1.

2.

3.

4.

5.

Be Proactive

Create rules on how your priorities will impact your decisions. A list of priorities without defined rules will limit their value. For instance, people who put faith as a top priority may believe Sunday is a day of rest. This value causes some entrepreneurs to keep their businesses closed on Sundays. This choice can also contribute to a desire to dedicate at least one day a week to family or personal self-care.

Another proactive strategy is to create a problem-response structure for your business. As you hire and develop trusted employees, you should delegate some decision-making responsibilities. Communicate which types of problems or situations should cause your team to contact you during your "non-work" time. The last thing you want is someone ruining your vacation because the printer stopped working. If you develop a clear and effective problem-response plan with empowered staff, that will guard against someone calling you over a $50 decision.

Minimize Distractions

Don't start your day checking e-mail because you'll be working on someone else's agenda and not your own. Minimizing unnecessary distractions is key to accomplishing your priorities. Mute notifications on all devices and avoid checking your phone or opening your work e-mails during time you set aside for your work projects. Keep conference calls short, not more than 30 minutes no matter who it is. Teach your spouse, kids, and friends not to make non-emergency personal calls to you during work hours.

Make Time for Yourself and Your Family

You know it's coming up. Spring break, summer vacation, Labor Day weekend, and then there are holidays. Your kids are clamoring for a vacation, or if you have no kids, it's time to get away with your significant other or your close friends. No matter how busy you are, your mental health demands some break time. But you need to make a plan for it so that your business can handle you being away.

Tip 1: Plan Ahead

Make vacations part of your annual planning calendar. As soon as the school calendar comes out and your spouse's obligations are clear. Plan special getaways and decide how you will spend certain holidays. Let your staff and clients know when you'll be out of town, so you can get orders completed or projects assigned before heading out. Do your best to clear your plate of work so that you can walk out the door confident that you didn't leave any critical activities undone. The best kind of vacations are laptop-free vacations. You need to really unplug to clear your mind and enjoy yourself. This will also help you transition back to work relaxed with a clear head, ready to dig in. A vacation often can spark some new ideas and you'll keep yourself from having a giant pile of work after your well-deserved time off.

Tip 2: Put Someone in Charge

If you want to see how well you've trained your team, find a replacement for yourself for the week you are on vacation. At the minimum, you need to delegate sales inquiries or customer service issues to points of contact that you can include in your out-of-office e-mail. You want people to know where they can get immediate help while you are out. Make sure the person you put in charge is confident in handling things while you're out. Go over any protocols or FAQs with your team to anticipate any questions or customer issues that could arise. This will discourage them from contacting you unless it's a true emergency. For your part, try not to call in more than once a day. You want to empower them to make decisions in your absence.

Tip 3: Schedule Your Marketing

What I love about digital marketing tools these days is how you can schedule your newsletters, social media updates, and blog posts in advance. No one even needs to know you're not working! Carve out time from your busy schedule to get your next few newsletters drafted, social media posts written, and blogs scheduled ahead of time, so everything can keep moving along and building your brand while you're out.

Tip 4: Tie Up Loose Ends

Do you have bills due while you're out? Most of your recurring bills should be on automatic draft, as late payments are the cause of the biggest drop in a credit scores. Pin down any pending meetings on your calendar for the end of the week you return. Make sure payroll is handled in advance, and that all vendor payments are scheduled or checks are signed and ready to be mailed while you are away. The more details you pay attention to ahead of time, the more relaxed you can be while you are away.

Tip 5: Relax. Your Business Will Be Fine

More than all the tactical stuff, this is the hardest thing for many business owners. Don't think that your business will fall apart if you're not there. The truth is, if you train your employees, they can handle it, whether you're a solopreneur or have a capable team. If you've empowered your employees or virtual assistant to handle most situations and you've done your part to clear your plate, you can go relax and enjoy your time off.

True balance may be unlikely for an entrepreneur until your business is much more mature than it is now, but if you focus on having quality experiences and being present for your team, your loved ones, and taking time for your self-care, it is certainly doable. You just have to re-frame your thinking and take the pressure off. For people with one job and a paycheck every two weeks, it's possible to have work/life balance. But you have ten jobs, all at one time, so it's not as easy for you. By carving out priorities, focusing on your top five activities each day, empowering your team to make decisions, and minimizing distractions, you can get a lot more done in your business, and stop feeling like you are running with your hair on fire trying to figure out what's burning.

EXPERT INTERVIEW

Lessons in Reigniting Your Purpose in Your Small Business

Candid interview with small business expert and author Barry Moltz

Have you ever felt like you lost your purpose in business and had to turn things around?
There are many times I have lost my way in my purpose in business. At that time, I ask the same three questions: "Who can I help the most?" "What do I love doing?" and "What am I the best at?" When I find where these answers intersect, I always get back on track.

What are the most common challenges small businesses face?
There are three common challenges in small business. First, owners don't have a consistent process for attracting and retaining customers. They go through a feast and famine cycle where they don't have enough business so they furiously do marketing. But once they get new customers, they stop doing any marketing so they can service those customers. In this way, they are never able to build a sustainable business.

The second biggest challenge is hiring people to leverage their time. So many small business owners only trust themselves to do the key tasks at their company. However, this leads to a job, not a growing business.

The final challenge is around managing the money in their company. Most don't have the knowledge and are afraid to learn how to read their financial statements. The problem is that if they don't know where the cash is going, they won't understand how to grow their company.

You've heard me say many times, that your book, *Bounce! Failure, Resiliency, and Confidence to Achieve Your Next Great*

Success, changed my life and my business. Can you explain what lessons you teach in it?

In *Bounce! Failure, Resiliency, and Confidence to Achieve Your Next Great Success*, I teach how to accept all outcomes. If something bad happens, then cheer the darkness. Learn what you can. Feel sad for yourself, but then let go after a day and move on. Don't wallow in the failure and search for answers. When this is done, take another action that can give you another chance at success.

What are your three top strategies for managing stress in the business?

The only way small business owners should manage stress is to decide each day what their top priorities are and do those first. They need to turn off all the other distractions that get in the way of being productive, not just busy. Quarterly, they should look into the future to plan where they are going, but daily, they need to work on what is in front of them and not think about all the possible things they could do in their business. It becomes too overwhelming.

What is your best advice for helping a business owner get unstuck?

My best advice for getting unstuck is to first identify what is holding the business back. Choose one area to fix first. It is usually one of these five:

1. New customer acquisition or retention.

2. Hiring and retaining the best employees.

3. Managing money.

4. Being productive, not just busy.

5. Improving the customer experience.

Now here is the first step to take in each of these areas:

1. New customer acquisition or retention: Do content marketing weekly so the company is there when customers are ready to buy.

2. Hiring and retaining the best employees: Hire for attitude fit, not skills. Delegate real responsibility to those that get hired.

3. Managing money: Work with the accountant to learn to understand your financial statements monthly.

4. Be productive, not just busy: The day before, decide the two things that need to get done first the next day before doing anything else.

5. Improving the customer experience: Ask customers why they do business with the company on an ongoing basis.

Barry Moltz has founded and run small businesses with a great deal of success and failure for more than 20 years. He now gets small businesses unstuck. He is the author of five best-selling small business books including his latest *How to Get Unstuck: 25 Ways to Get Your Business Growing Again*. For more information, go to www.barrymoltz.com.

FIX YOUR PURPOSE

EMERSON'S URGENCIES: **SEEK HELP IMMEDIATELY!**
• If you are about to lose your spouse and family because you devote too much time to the business.
What steps can you take to be a better partner? 1. 2. 3. 4. 5.
What is your business purpose?
Can you renew it now and commit to the future?
If you are unsure of your purpose, brainstorm some reasons "Why" you are in business: What does your purpose mean for your vision?

FIX YOUR BUSINESS ACTION STEPS

Take these steps and add your own based on Chapter 2: PURPOSE.

1. Share your PURPOSE with your team this week. Get their feedback and make revisions if needed for clarity.

2. Share your renewed VISION with your team this week. Get their feedback and make revisions if needed for clarity.

3. Have you got your ego under control? If not, make a plan to work on that. If you really can't see your challenge, it might be good to consult a professional coach or therapist.

4. Start using the Top 5 daily task list to prioritize your day.

5. Practice being a family-first entrepreneur. Schedule a surprise special evening for your partner or family.

CHAPTER 3: PEOPLE
GETTING THE RIGHT TEAM AND ADVISORS

I once had an HR manager tell me, "If you have people there is a potential for problems." I think this is true, but in business you need employees to grow. Being a one-man army gets old fast. When it comes to looking at the people issues in your business, there are four key things to consider: whether you need people, whether you have the right or wrong people, how you train your people, and whether your leadership (or lack thereof) is driving your people or customers away. Let's start with leadership.

Leadership vs. Management

When you own a business, you're automatically both a leader and a manager. However, having the responsibilities of a business leader doesn't necessarily make a person an effective leader. Being a leader and manager are two completely different roles. Managers are facilitators of their team members' success. A leader can be anyone on the team who has a particular talent, great idea, or industry experience that can prove useful to the team. The best managers consistently allow different leaders to emerge and inspire their team and themselves to reach for the next level. You will need to grow your leadership skills to grow your business.

Now is the time to figure out what kind of leader and manager you have been and what kind you want to be going forward. Your ideal management style will depend on what kind of business you run, the specific business challenge you face, your industry, your personality, and the people you choose to help you reach your business goals.

Your Management Style

The labels we give to different management styles evolve, but you probably recognize most of them. Some business owners are visionary leaders. They give the big picture vision or strategic direction for the business and let the team figure out the "How" of it. Visionary leaders help others see the overarching goal and stay focused on it.

Then there's the coercive leader who simply tells employees what to do, when to do it, and how to do it. This leader rules with an iron fist by ordering and dictating, even demeaning his/her employees at times when everything is not executed perfectly. When you use coercive leadership, your employees feel a lack of responsibility toward their work and little accountability. They will only do what they are told to do.

Pace-setting leaders expect a lot from employees and model excellence and self-direction. This high energy leader won't ask anyone to do what they're not willing to do themselves. They push people hard, but they work just as hard or harder right alongside the team to earn the respect of the team.

Autocratic leaders provide clear expectations and focus on always having a commanding presence. These leaders put a lot of pressure on themselves to make all the decisions on their own. The autocratic approach can be a good thing when the situation calls for a rapid decision and decisive action. This style of leadership works best when the team is young and inexperienced.

Democratic leaders like a collaborative environment and encourage all team members to participate in decision-making.

This type of leader reserves the right to make final decisions, but they use team input to arrive at their opinion.

Coaching leaders are managers who work one-on-one with team members to encourage their confidence and professional development. And when their employees don't deliver, they first consider how they could have better set their employees up for success. Employees love this approach. Coaching can inspire fierce loyalty, as well as driven and satisfied employees.

All these leadership approaches can work in a business. The key thing to understand about leadership is that it will need to adjust to the needs of the people you are leading. Typically, you don't have just one style. Your leadership style should be adapted to the business situation and the people involved.

Is your current management style working? Or do you have high turnover among your team? Have you considered that your leadership might be the issue? Now's the time to reconsider your approach. Here's a Personal Fix.

Personal FIX
Your Management Style

How many leadership styles do you have
in your tool belt?

Rate your leadership styles from 1 to 5, with 5 being strongest.

Visionary: Visionary leaders articulate where the business is going. _____

Coercive: Coercive leaders make demands and require immediate compliance with orders. _____

Democratic: Democratic leaders engage their team in major business decisions. _____

Pace-setting: Pace-setting leaders inspire excellence and expect self-direction. _____

Autocratic: Autocratic leaders make expectations known and make all decisions. _____

Coaching: Coaching leaders develop the individual strengths of the team. _____

Could you benefit from leadership training? If so, sign up for a leadership development course.

Developing Your People Processes

However autocratic, democratic, or hands-off your management style, you will need to master many skills in your role as a business leader. It's your job to decide when to hire, and whom to hire, and for what roles they will serve. It's your job to make sure they have the right processes and tools to do their jobs, and that they understand the big picture of your purpose and vision. It's also your job to make certain they are motivated to serve your customers happily and capably. Your employees represent your brand with excellence. Your job is to hold them accountable, help them when they're struggling, and fire them when they can't or won't measure up despite your best efforts to train them.

Plus, it's your responsibility to build a company culture that reflects your purpose and is consistent with your values. You need a team culture where everyone can find a place. You need team members who can do their best work within your personal management style.

Construct the Best Team Using Your Management Skills

Putting together a great team naturally requires the right mix of skills among team members. However, there are times when someone with exceptional skills simply isn't right for a role due to poor soft skills or lack of ability to collaborate well with others. You're generally better off choosing the person with good skills and excellent cultural fit than the outright prodigy who can't get along with people. Skills can be improved upon, but it's hard to teach people to be nice. That was their mother's job.

Understanding human nature and ego is also critical when putting together your dream team. Team members should be willing to accept great ideas no matter who they come from. You should also be willing to share your own mistakes and learn from them. Creating the perfect team for your business may require doing things in an unorthodox manner, but that's fine. Trying new things can often produce breakthrough moments that make your business more competitive.

As an outstanding manager, your job is to take people's talents and translate them into exceptional performance. To do this requires you to understand each team member's strengths and weaknesses and to find ways to challenge each person to transcend expectations and achieve consistent, excellent performance. It's also necessary for you to understand their personal and professional goals and how you can encourage those alongside your business objectives.

"Good Management" Depends on Your Business

What you do and what industry you're in influence what "good management" means. That doesn't mean you must buy ping pong tables and video games for your office, or that your buttoned-up law firm can't be a fun place for people to work. Just be certain your management style is part of a coherent strategy that considers organizational goals, individual needs, your business culture, and your team's strengths and weaknesses.

You want to decide the business dress code. Is it formal, business casual, or are jeans OK? Consider your policy on work hours. Will you allow flex hours, working from home, or summer hours? What perks will you offer? In my business, we close the office the last two weeks of the year and pay everyone for the holidays, so no one takes any vacation time. If you have more of a virtual team or consultants that you pull in as needed, how will you build a cohesive team?

Everyone who works for you needs to work together seamlessly and present a united front to your clients. Try regular weekly staff calls or meetings and utilize collaboration software like Teamwork, Basecamp, or Slack to help keep everyone on the same page and with access to all critical files.

Ready to Stop the High Churn of Employees?

Are you tired of seeing your employees churn through your business and leave your company after six months or less? Sorry to say, but it might be a lack of structure, training, or how you handle your staff that's causing them to leave. It's your job as the business owner and manager to adopt managerial habits that will help you have a strong, effective company with happy, motivated employees.

Listen

When employees vent, do you get caught up in their words or do you really try to hear the underlying problem? If they are unhappy, and it's a reasonable request, do your best to fix it. If an employee's issues have started to affect their attitude, you need to fix the problem before it spreads to the rest of your team or that employee hands in her notice. Of course, there are chronic complainers, but there could be some truth in every complaint.

Let your employees know they can speak to you candidly. When they do come to you, make sure you have your listening ears on. Sometimes they want a problem solved; other times, they just want a sympathetic ear. Figure out which they want and act accordingly.

Support

Many entrepreneurs think that support is a one-way street, in that employees support the business and not the other way around. Understand that you have an important relationship with your employees and, if you foster it properly, you can create satisfied employees that help your business grow quickly.

Consider how you can support your team. Educational development, unscheduled time off, and financial incentives can show that you care about each of your employees and make them feel more invested in contributing their all to your business.

Focus on Professional Development

Employee development sounds like it must be expensive, but it can be done simply, too. It can include paying for an online course, setting up an informal book club, sharing thoughts on the latest developments in your industry, or even a lunch-time lecture from one employee to the rest of the team.

It is important to give each employee the chance to shine by sharing his or her knowledge, passions, or hobbies. Your receptionist can teach your team about using the project management software more effectively, or your lead designer could share how to enjoy her favorite hobby—knitting—in the break room over bagels and coffee.

Nurture

Offering your staff an environment where they can develop discipline, foster growth, and cultivate sustainable habits will help them grow with your company. Do your best to treat your employees as equals, not minions, and encourage their capacity to grow. If you know an employee has outgrown his current position, don't hold him back; consider him for a promotion or give him additional responsibilities.

Appreciation Goes a Long Way

I'm a big fan of hand-written notes that let employees know you see their hard work. Gestures and words of appreciation always brighten someone's day. While I'm sure the creator of Administrative Professionals' Day had her heart in the right place, celebrations of this sort can feel hollow if the boss is unpleasant the other 259 days of the work year.

Build appreciation into the culture of your company. While buying a cake for the birthday boy in the office may seem fun (unless that person is on a diet), instead, let the employee choose how to celebrate their special day. Stick a Post-it note on a staffer's desk with a cheery show of appreciation. Give your staff a half-day off after they've met a particularly grueling deadline.

Keeping employees motivated and working hard for you doesn't necessarily require that you pay them the highest salary in town. It's the small, thoughtful ways you show that you are paying attention to your team that help them become loyal to you and keep them motivated.

How to Hire Help

Before you go and hire anyone, you have some housekeeping to take care of. If you're still operating as a Sole Proprietor, it's time to establish a more appropriate business structure. There's just so much legal and financial liability when you are a solopreneur, especially when you start hiring employees. Go to FixYourBusiness.com for resources on how to incorporate your business inexpensively online. Or find a local attorney who specializes in serving small businesses to assist you. Try your local Small Business Development Center or SCORE chapter for legal recommendations as well.

From your very first hire through your 100th, you want to attract the kind of employees who will be an asset to your company. You want hard-working, conscientious individuals who won't cause you to break the bank to hire them. But it goes deeper than that. Hiring employees requires plenty of planning and reflection to understand your staffing needs, your management style, and the kind of company culture you want to build.

Consider Your Hiring Options

Full-time isn't your only option here. If your budget is small, bringing on full-timers might be further down the road. You can also consider the following options:

Virtual Workers

You have the option to hire staff who work "virtually" from their homes. Many small business owners hire virtual assistants, who work as contractors for part-time hours, instead of taking on an employee.

Virtual assistants are experienced admins or stay-at-home moms coming back into the workforce. You can find them by referral, from an online source, or job board. (Check out FixYourBusiness.com for resources.) They provide services like receptionist, scheduler, database management, email/newsletter management, copy editing, bookkeeping, proposal formatting, social media management, and other time-saving and life-saving chores that keep you focused on doing things that grow your business!

Even if you have a virtual assistant doing back-office support tasks, if you have a business where customers come and go or products are made, stored, delivered, or shipped, then you need W-2 employees too.

Part-Time Employees

A part-time staff member typically works 10 to 30 hours a week, and you aren't required to pay health benefits for them. One perk of utilizing part-time help is that you can adjust worker schedules to reflect the needs of your business. The downside is people want a consistent schedule and fewer people are looking for part-time roles.

Temporary Workers

Usually you would hire a temp worker through a staffing agency. They're ideal if you need help for a few weeks or months, as you can let them go and get another worker immediately if they are not performing or when your busy season is over. Another advantage of this option is if you do like the worker, you can offer him/her a permanent or contract position to stay on with your firm.

Independent Contractors

Working with freelancers or "1099" independent contractors can help with business needs that don't require direct supervision such as graphic design, business analyst, sales, project management, copy writing, website development, or handling your accounting. You don't pay social security or payroll taxes for contractors. But, understand that the IRS has a strict interpretation of what they define as an independent contractor. The general rule is that an individual is an independent contractor if the business has the right to direct only the result of the work and not when and how the work will be done. You cannot label a worker as an independent contractor if the where, when, and how the work is done is controlled by the business owner.

One advantage of using contractors is that you can test out how you like them, without the expense of bringing them on as an official employee. Some people like being contractors and running their own business. If you like their work, your business can become one of their regular customers or you can hire them full-time and make them an asset to your business.

Interns

A cost-friendly staffing option is hiring interns. An internship is a temporary work experience for a college student that focuses on providing relevant knowledge and skills in a specific field. They can be paid, unpaid, or partially paid. Call the career office at a local college to advertise for a student intern who's studying in your field. I am a big fan of hiring co-op students because they typically will stay with your company three to six months. Sometimes interns are only available over the summer. I also like to hire recent grads as interns who maybe need more experience on their résumé. An internship is an audition for a real job. If you like their work, you can always hire them or make them an offer upon graduation to come back and join the company.

Pre FIX
Know the Hiring Rules

1. Learn the difference between a W-2 employee and a 1099 contractor before you hire. Ask your accountant or HR consultant to clarify. Never bend these rules!
2. The days of college interns being "paid" in college credit instead of real dollars are pretty much over. If you need an intern to do work, that intern should be paid.
3. At some point, you should become an employee of your company, and collect a regular paycheck, if you don't already. Some legal entities don't allow this, but talk with your accountant, and if you can, get this set up.
4. Your job descriptions and interview language must comply with the Americans with Disabilities Act and Fair Labor Standards Act.
5. Take the time to write down your interview questions so that you ask all candidates the same questions for each position.

Know What You Need

Pinpoint exactly the skill sets you need to round out your team. Each person should have a slightly different background and experience so that they complement one another. But really drill down into your needs. Do you need to hire someone who has copy editing skills, understands social media, or online advertising? What specific social platforms do they need to know? The more you know about your needs, the better you can attract the right job candidates.

List the Key Job Tasks

Before you write the job description, start by simply brain-storming an exhaustive list of tasks you need executed in the position. Initially, your list may be helter-skelter, with some admin tasks, some marketing, some finance, and so on. But as you complete the list, start to sort them into categories so you can determine what type of role you need to hire for. Then, prioritize those job tasks so you can tackle the most important ones with your first hire.

It's helpful to divide this list into categories. Each job description you put together will likely include some of each:

- Critical tasks
- Routine tasks
- Occasional tasks

Write Your Job Description

Now that you've defined the tasks you need from your next employee, organize them into separate jobs. This is important so that you're not trying to recruit an amazing admin who not only can file, but can also do your taxes, manage your social media, give you a manicure, and run your IT department!

Consider what qualifications your new employee must have to do the job. Do you require a high school or college graduate? An associate degree or BS in Marketing? How much previous experience should the new employee have? Keep in mind, a person who only has partial credentials may not be qualified to do the job satisfactorily. Now is the time to be precise, especially if you are hiring your first or second employee.

Organize your thoughts into a job description. The more detailed your job description, the more likely you will be to find exactly the right fit for the role you need to fill. I like to write down everything that the employee could possibly be asked to do so that there are no surprises down the road.

Start Your Search

Once you have a job description and a salary range, look in as many places as possible to maximize your search. Before you hit the job boards, let everyone know you're hiring, since referrals are an excellent source for great employees. Ask your social network for referrals, too. I've had great success recruiting through my social media profiles.

Also, post a notice in your company newsletter. Referral candidates can be cheaper to hire, faster to get on board, and have a retention rate of 46% after being at a company for one year.

Once you ask your colleagues, friends, employees, and business contacts if they know of a candidate that would be a good fit for your company, then determine who will handle the initial screening of applicants before posting a listing on an online job referral site. If you have a friend who works in HR this might be a good opportunity to ask for some help to develop an approach for this employee search. Keep in mind, when you post on online job boards you could be overwhelmed with the number of résumés from candidates. There are three main places to source employees:

- Job boards
- LinkedIn
- Recruiters

Interviewing and Selecting an Employee

If you've never hired employees before, or if you've made some poor hiring decisions in the past, it's probably because you just didn't develop a hiring process. As busy business owners, we hire people because we need someone fast, or they need a job, or just because we like them. Ok, I'll admit it—once upon a time

I hired people this way, which is why I share this advice now. If you haven't checked out a candidate's references, or given them any skills tests, you don't know if they can do the job or would be a good culture fit. Your interview process needs to change, so that you have the best opportunity to find an employee who will be with your company for a significant amount of time.

As you think through your hiring process, answer these questions: How big of a pool of applicants will you need to review? Where will you source applicants? Who will do the first screening of résumés? Will you do phone interviews or written interviews, in addition to in-person interviews? If you don't know how to conduct a good interview or involve others in the interview process, you won't get the information you need to make the best hiring decision. Ask a business mentor or hire an HR consultant to help you, if you're not sure how to conduct a formal interview process.

When you spend the time up front developing a hiring process and a detailed job description to identify the type of employee you need, you should be rewarded with an employee who will help you take your business to the next level.

What's Your Onboarding Process?

Turnover is expensive. The cost of replacing an entry-level employee is 30 to 50 percent of the person's annual salary. And every time someone leaves, morale and productivity suffer across the company, especially if you have a small team. That's why it's vital that all businesses hold on to their people. It starts by providing a well-designed onboarding process to educate new employees about their place within the culture and the company. It's not just about completing the employee verification paperwork, establishing benefits, an e-mail address, and assigning a key card.

The more time you spend training new employees, the better they will perform in your company. You should plan on conducting two to four weeks of training for any new employee. The more training materials and processes you have set up, the faster a new hire will learn and feel acclimated to your company. Your goal is to set your new employee up to be a highly productive member of your team. You need to have general training materials for your company, as well as those specific to the role you're hiring for.

If you plan to work with a freelancer or agency, use project management software to give them access to all the pertinent documents, login info, and details they need to be successful at helping you with the projects they are assigned.

Ask your key employees to create documentation quarterly of tasks they perform and vendors used. This will help you cross-train employees and make sure you are not handicapped by the sudden departure or illness of any key employee. This will help you maintain momentum as your business grows.

Culture Fit Can be a Struggle

For the first time in modern history, the workforce consists of four and sometimes five generations within a single company. That age/experience difference can lead to varied ways of looking at things as coworkers work with those from another generation. The generation gaps can show up in communication styles, goals, adaptation to change, and technical skills. Encourage new employees to build bridges by investing the time to learn about their coworkers and their motivations. Despite wide age disparities, common ground needs to be found.

Be visible and check-in every couple of days after you've hired a new team member. Don't assume people you're mentoring haven't asked a question because they already know the answer. Be proactive about giving them a chance to share their thoughts and ask questions. Encourage open feedback and do your best to remove any obstacles he/she might be experiencing. Set clear expectations for projects and business goals. No matter what generation your workers are from, you should make sure each employee understands exactly what you want or need, and how you want it done with a specific deadline.

Sharing your company vision is important for engagement. Share a big enough "Why" story with new employees to keep them motivated. Younger employees want to feel like they are a part of something bigger than themselves. Your "Why" is essentially the core values of the company culture. Some business owners are put off by a new employee's need to know the "Why" for the things they're asked to do, but do not be offended, just realize that they are wired differently. Once your rules and methods are explained and they understand their role in the success of the company, everybody can move forward with a renewed purpose.

Once you've done this successfully with new hires, make it your road map for future additions to your team.

Learn What Works Best

Use time with employees wisely. Observation can go a long way in identifying employee strengths and weaknesses, but it isn't sufficient. One terrific way to learn more about employee strengths is to ask, "What was your best day at work in recent memory?" Ask what they were doing, and why that day was considered the best. You may identify potential as well as existing strengths, which is also valuable information.

And though you may have an idea of employee weaknesses, asking about their *worst* day at work in recent memory can be revealing. Weaknesses aren't necessarily things that people aren't good at, but things that frustrate them or that they find unrewarding. Sometimes those weaknesses can be turned into strengths.

Frustration indicates a need for change, or that the person feels they've outgrown a specific job task. It can also indicate that the employee is not a team player or willing to do their job anymore. Culture fit is more important than skill set. You can teach someone to do any position, but you can't teach people to respect their teammates. When considering your team's strengths and weaknesses, be a good listener, and look for ways to keep employees motivated.

Performance Review Process

Your employees deserve to know how you will evaluate their job performance, and what constitutes satisfactory performance. You also need to give them a path for how they can improve, and how they can earn more opportunity and/or higher pay, if those things are even possible in your company.

You need to have a system to review their performance fairly and routinely. It doesn't have to be complicated, but it must be legal and you should put your decisions in writing each year to be filed in that employee's confidential personnel file. Present your evaluation in person, give the employee the opportunity to respond—in writing if he/she wishes—and both of you should sign a written record of your conversation.

As your company continues to grow and you employ managers who are evaluating other employees, be sure that your performance review procedures grow with you! There are many methods that you can study to find one that fits your culture, your business, your management style, and your personal values. The keys are fairness and consistency.

Team FIX
Do you have the right team to grow your business?

- Do they get along with one another?
- Are they productive enough?
- Do you enjoy working with each of your employees?
- Is anyone making consistent mistakes?
- Does drama get in the way of any of them taking care of business?
- Does your team energize or drain your energy?

1. Deal with any individual employee issues, individually.
2. Ask these questions again.
3. If you are not satisfied with team dynamics, engage them in team-building activities.

Doer/Thinker Ratio

Your first employee you will most likely be what I call a "doer." They will do what you ask them to do to take some heat off you. Some employees like to have clear directions for their job and then dig in and get things done. They are very focused on accomplishing the tasks at hand and thrive on activity. You can't live without doers in a business. But you need someone in your business thinking about how your business makes money, other than you.

"Thinker" employees are more analytical. Not only can they do things, they solve problems. They can figure out how to get things done and even kick around a new strategy with you. As a seasoned professional, they may push back or resist being told exactly how you want things done, but if they get results that shouldn't matter. Just tell them the outcome and let them do it their way.

As you build your team, you need both. But I recommend a ratio of three-to-one doers to thinkers. The average small business has six employees, so two thinkers can work. You need at least one thinker, other than you, who can help you plan for growth, implement new sales strategies, make strategic decisions, and mull over all kinds of choices about what to do next. But you also need a strong base of doers to get stuff done.

It Might Be Time to Clean House

It's not personal; it's business. If there's anyone on your team who you feel is deterring your business from its true potential, let them go. That sounds harsh, but sometimes we put up with poor behavior from employees because it just seems easier than finding a replacement. It could be a control freak employee who hoards information from other employees to keep power, or maybe your best sales person brings in the business but is an 800-pound gorilla who is mean to everyone. You should not put up with bullies in your workplace who don't value teammates. Hold yourself accountable here: your goal is to create a team that works well together for your business, and if someone isn't in line with that objective, it's time to get rid of them.

Create a Team Culture

You must intentionally create the culture for your business. This is a challenge for me at times because my marketing/sales/operations team is primarily virtual, so it's not like we're chatting over coffee in the break room each day. However, I strive to create cohesion by having a weekly team call. I also do an annual team retreat at the beginning of the year where I fly in the team and plan out our year. This is our chance to check in with one another, catch up a bit on the personal stuff, and make sure we're aligned in what's happening with SmallBizLady Enterprises and Quintessence Group, my marketing consulting firm. Since I run two companies, it can be a challenge, but everyone enjoys connecting.

If your team is all physically in the same location, it should be fairly easy to build and foster that team culture. Hold regular staff meetings so that people who may work on their own can feel like they are a part of something greater. Take them out to lunch. Periodically schedule conversations to stay connected with everyone individually. Show them that you care about them personally and that you want them to feel like they belong.

Leverage technology like Skype so you can be "face-to-face" and try to plan an event not related to work where you meet in real time at some point during the year. You'd be amazed at how spending time together and not just talking about work can really strengthen your bond.

You rely on your staff to help your business grow. So naturally you want a team that enjoys working together. Get clear on what you want in a team, and make sure the people you employ are always living up to your expectations. It starts with making sure they know what you expect, training them regularly, and then holding them accountable.

Retaining Top Talent

Even if you follow the guidelines on how to hire your first employee or the best practices for hiring and interviewing candidates, employees typically decide in the first six months if they will stay around. It's not just poor workers who will affect how your team pool changes. Millennials, who comprise the largest generation currently working, and represent nearly 50% of today's workforce, have exhibited a trend of job-hopping in search of the best job with the highest compensation.

The goal for you, as a small business owner, is to prevent your most talented employees from jumping ship. You need your employees and they need you, too. You will run across your fair share of bad employees during your time as an entrepreneur, but when you begin adding valuable, talented employees to your team, you need to know how to hold on to them. It will be the best thing you can do for your business. Here are some tips for how to retain your best and brightest employees.

1. Think Long-Term

If it's financially impossible to increase an employee's compensation, you need to remind him/her that one day it *will* be. Be sure that all your employees have a concrete idea of what your vision is for your business and what role they'll play in helping you get there. Make them understand why you do what you do. If you voice how much you believe in yourself and your team, the desire to stay working for you and helping you reach that goal will follow. If you treat your employees well, they'll trust you enough to know that when you become successful, so will they.

2. Compensate Fairly

Depending on the skill and education levels you require for your position, compensation will play a large role in obtaining and *keeping* talented people in your business. A paycheck and its accompanying benefits is a huge factor when workers consider leaving for another employer. Do you offer health benefits, a retirement package, or an annual review during which good work is rewarded with a raise? You should consider these things and figure out compensation that is fair so you can keep your best employees.

3. Give Perks

While small business owners have the desire to compensate employees very well, we all know money can get in the way. If you can't financially afford to pay your employees exactly what they deserve, figure out what else you can do to balance the scale. Sculpt a laidback, but professional, work culture where creativity and inter-office friendships are encouraged. Offer paid vacations and sick days, maternity and paternity leave, or allow them the use of your equipment for a side project. If you feel that your employees might deserve more than what they see in their paychecks, there's no harm in offering them other benefits.

4. Offer Growth Opportunities

Talented employees crave responsibility and growth. If you're sure an employee is someone you want to keep on your team, offer him/her the opportunity to take on more challenging and engaging work. This will keep your employee interested while also preventing the job from becoming mundane or predictable. Keep your talented employees on their toes with more demands. They will see and feel the trust and faith you have in them and work harder.

How Will You Handle HR Going Forward?

Once you have clearly defined procedures for hiring employees, bringing them onboard, training them, managing their benefits, assessing their performance, determining their rate of pay or salary increases, how promotions and dismissals are handled, then you are well on your way to having a business employer brand.

As your business grows though, you'll need to develop a formal Human Resources function in the company. That could involve hiring an employee to handle human resources or an HR consultant, but you won't be able to do it all alone. Eventually you'll need to update your employee handbook to communicate important workplace changes to employees and demonstrate compliance with various employment laws. It's a best practice to review your handbook at least annually to ensure it is up to date with current laws and company procedures.

If there is an inconsistency in what employees are experiencing on the job, your run the risk of disengagement and poor employee morale, not to mention a potential lawsuit. The way you handle business operations is governed by a lot of employment law—not just good will and common sense—so it's very important that you seek reliable guidance whenever you are making personnel decisions. With federal tax reform, expanded overtime regulations, gender pay equality, and paid sick leave laws expanding across the country, human resources can no longer just be something you should guess at for your business.

One low-cost source of help is a professional payroll service, which can not only manage your payroll checks, taxes, and unemployment insurance payments, but can often provide background checks, aptitude testing, sample job descriptions, draft employee handbooks, and the required employee notification posters for your place of business. Many payroll services also offer HR consulting services and call-in lines where you can get answers to pressing HR questions.

Please visit FixYourBusiness.com for resources to manage the people side of your business.

Who Advises You Outside Your Business?

Smart business owners have a few key advisors to help them make strategic decisions about their company. When your business is still small and you probably don't have outside investors other than family and friends, you can pull together what I like to call your "kitchen cabinet of advisors." This is a group of informal advisors—and unlike an official board—they will work for food. The price of lunch is all you pay for their advice in most cases.

Your cabinet should include around five people, including an existing entrepreneur, a customer or potential customer, and a mentor—all who have business expertise to lend. You should also try to include a lawyer and an accountant in your kitchen cabinet. If you had the opportunity to go to college you probably know someone who is an accountant or an attorney. You might even include your spouse if he or she has a good temperament and some business experience to contribute. And if you're fortunate to be housed in a co-working space or business incubator, take advantage of all mentors available there.

This is a confidential sounding board of people who are invested in your success. But you must be careful with how you leverage these advisors, because if you ask for advice, and then don't take it, you could damage these relationships. And don't just talk by phone with your advisors, get them together in person a few times a year. They might like to meet and network with each other.

Expert Interview

How to Have Better People Management in Your Small Business

Candid interview with human resource consultant and author Oginga Carr

What are the biggest hiring mistakes small business owners make?

The biggest issue with hiring in small businesses is the lack of a system. Many of us fly by the seat of our pants when selecting our employees and that can be a fatal flaw. We need to be more duty-centric in the hiring process. It all starts with developing a great job description. What are the bona fide occupational qualifications of the job? What are the essential skills and competencies that are necessary? By developing a system for hiring based upon the job description, we can be open about our expectations with the applicant and have better qualified prospects.

When should you start developing a hiring process in your business?

Hiring processes should be developed the moment that you start adding employees to your organization. We would like to set up a process to create what I like to call 'core employees.' A core employee is defined as an employee who has been with your organization for 2 years or more. Once someone is a core employee, they have a high level of efficiency. Studies show it costs three times the salary of a core employee to replace that core employee with another core employee. So, if we develop a proper hiring process, we can have more core employees, which lessens the cost on the bottom line.

There is a war for good, qualified people. How can a small business compete without a major benefits package?

We are able to attract good, qualified people to our organization by being clear in our brand narrative. People will stay at an organization where they are happy. Therefore, during the hiring process, while it is important to be duty centric, it is also important to be clear about the mission of the organization. We must find people who are interested in our mission. You can't pay your employees enough money to be happy. It is about finding those mission-based reasons and non-cash incentives that motivate your employees to stay.

How can business owners set up new employees for success?
How do I spell success? T-R-A-I-N-I-N-G. We do not invest enough in our most valuable assets: our employees. We must immerse our new employees in the training, coaching, and mentorship within our organization; it fast tracks their success in the organization. With the proper hiring process, we should know that they have the skill set to do the job. Now when they start within the organization we should be able to give them five goals for success at their position. We should be able to quantify what success looks like and then give them a road map to get there. The biggest issue in employee retention is communication. The next issue is engagement. By keeping your employees engaged in their work and in the environment, we set them up for success.

What are the main advantages and disadvantages of using contractors?
Contractors can be a gift and a curse. It is great to have competent professionals who can step in and take on projects that you need to get completed quickly so that you can focus on other tasks. Also, with contractors, we don't have to deal with any of the attachments of dealing with employees and the agreements are easily voided. On the other hand, there are inherent dangers when dealing with contractors. First, we have to be very clear in expectations in our contractor relationships or they can be legally considered employees, which carries hefty consequences. Plus, we have to be selective in the contractors we work with and make sure that they are as dedicated to the project and our business almost as much as we are. Ultimately,

if we can navigate those potential dangers, using contractors can be an excellent way to fast track success in our business.

Payroll and paperwork connected to payroll are major stumbling blocks for business owners. What can they do to mitigate risk?
Record retention is one of the more overlooked portions of our businesses. It all comes down to having a system. Start with access. Who is allowed to see sensitive and medical files? We should denote in the employee's job description which files, if any, they are allowed to see. Where do we keep the files? Sensitive and medical files are required to be kept at what is called the level of negligence; in a locked room and in a locked file cabinet. If we are keeping the files electronically, then they must be kept in a password protected folder. When do we get rid of the files? There are a few different retention periods, but the main issue is having a retention schedule and process for destroying records. Process is king. If you put together a structured process, it may mitigate the legal risks within your organization.

Do you have recommendations for outsourcing and managing a virtual team?
When it comes to outsourcing and managing a virtual team, you want to grow strategically. We should take our virtual employees through the same training process as our local employees. The key is technology. Using video chatting software can make your virtual team feel as close as your local team. It is also important to plan opportunities to meet with your virtual team in person periodically. You should definitely obtain references of work for your virtual staff. They must have a special skill set to complete the required work with minimal supervision.

What is your best advice for business owners who want to invest in new team members to grow the business?
Before you invest in new team members, be mission focused. What is the mission of your expansion? What results are you

searching for? By defining success, it gives us an idea what we are looking for. Too many times we embark on new projects without a real destination. We also need to know what the financial outlay is that we are willing to invest. There are four steps to successful teams: Mutual Purpose, Empowered People, Proper Change Communication, and Visionary Leadership. If we can have a purpose, empower our people to achieve that purpose, properly communicate the inevitable changes, and have a vision for our organization, we can develop successful teams that will accomplish the goals of the organization and grow.

About the Expert:

Oginga Carr is an author, national seminar leader, organizational structure expert, and Human Resource consultant. He brings 17 years of experience in sales, management, and organizational development. His passion is in the dynamic of change; dealing with it, working through it, and preparing for it. Oginga focuses on productivity through structure and human capital development. **Learn more at www.ogingacarr.com.**

FIX YOUR PEOPLE ISSUES

EMERSON'S URGENCIES: **SEEK HELP IMMEDIATELY!**
Do you have an employee who is wrong, wrong, wrong for the job, or a menace to you or other employees? Get help now! Write down the steps you can take to remove them: 1. 2. 3. 4. 5.
Have a candid conversation with your team about your company culture. Be sure you do more **listening** than talking. If you're not sure you can listen, invite a trained facilitator to lead this activity.
Do you know your leadership style(s)? Do you know the work styles of your team? Can you tell the doers from the thinkers? Make a list of your team, including you, and write down your impression of everyone's style of workplace behavior.
Jot down other ideas for how you will build a new onboarding process for employees.

FIX YOUR BUSINESS ACTION STEPS

Write down how you want to improve your human resource management based on Chapter 3: People. These plans will grow with you and your business.

ACTION STEP	DUE DATE
1. Research Legal Requirements for Hiring Employees	
2. Develop Hiring Process	
3. Develop Job Description(s)	
4. Develop Your Interview Process	
5. Update Compensation and Benefits Plans	
6. Design New Employee Intake Processes	
7. Develop Employee Onboarding Processes	
8. Create Performance Assessment and Review Process	
9. Establish Ongoing Training and Development Schedule	

CHAPTER 4: PROFIT
MANAGING YOUR MONEY

Let's face it, profit is how we keep score in business. It's not about what you make, it's about what you keep. In other words, gross revenue is what you make and net revenue is the profit left over after all the business expenses are paid. My business took off to heights I never imagined the moment I put a system in place around my finances – both in business and in my personal life. Before I had a system, money told me what to do, and often my personal finances took the hit.

For years, I was guaranteed to skip at least one paycheck a month to pay for something in my business. That all stopped when I made the decision that I was not living to work. I had to remind myself that I was working hard in my business in order to live my dream life. And what that meant was that I was no longer willing to skip paychecks. My family needed money, too.

When you work like a beast in your business and don't take a paycheck on a consistent basis something, or perhaps a few things, are wrong with your revenue model or cash flow management. You need a fix. Answer these questions below honestly to see where you are in managing your business finances.

Do any of these sound like you?

"Dang, it's payroll again this week?"

"We must pay this bill in advance to order inventory, the vendor won't extend us credit!"

"The loan payment is automatically deducted from the account weekly, and now we can't pay this other bill."

"This vendor has to wait on payment, we are still waiting on a check from the client."

If these are regular conversations you are having in your business, you must strengthen your cash flow management. This is too much stress and chaos, but I understand. I've been there. If everything coming in is just going back out, and you're not paying yourself regularly or putting any money away for your retirement, it's time to make a change. Let me help you Fix Your Business.

Mini FIX
In Search of Profit: Key Money Questions

Answer these questions:

- Are you more focused on revenue than profit?
- Do you have a profitable pricing model?
- Are you selling enough?
- Are you spending too much?
- Do you often have collections issues?
- Do you struggle to make payroll?
- Are you constantly struggling with cash flow management?

If your answers to three or more of these questions are negative, it's time to dig into the numbers in your business.

Establish Your Money Rules

Let's talk about establishing your money rules. In my business, I only pay vendors twice a month, regardless of when invoices are received. We do this to help with cash flow management. Another money rule we use is the first time we do business with a customer, we must have an electronic funds transfer or wire payment, we will not accept a check. Now it's time for you to set your money rules with this Pre FIX.

Pre FIX
Set Your Money Rules!

1. What forms of payment will you accept from customers? (ACH Wire, Credit Cards, Checks)
2. Do your contracts and invoices offer discounts for early payments? *(Note: Net 30 payments should never get a discount.)*
3. What is your policy on vendor payments?
4. How will you manage your collections process?
5. How will you collect upfront fees before starting projects?
6. How do you handle petty cash?
7. What is your business/travel reimbursement policy?
8. For what kinds of expenses will you draw down on the business line-of-credit?
9. Do you have a go/no-go checklist for business opportunities based on profitability of the deal?
10. When is skipping your paycheck off limits?

How often are you reviewing your financial statements? Don't let it be a surprise to you at tax time whether or not your business made any money. Lots of business owners don't fully understand the financial side of running their businesses and thus have no idea whether their business is profitable or losing money year over year. I don't know where you are in the financial management side of your business, but this chapter lays out my plan for *Stress-Free Finances*.

Now, as we go through this chapter, I am going to start at the beginning with accounting basics and you just feel free to jump in when I get to your stage. But if you are not actively managing not only the cash but the whole financial picture of your company, now and for the future, it won't hurt you to start right here.

Accounting — The Big Picture

All the details of money management in your business fall under the umbrella of accounting, which is defined as "the systematic process of identifying, recording, measuring, classifying, verifying, summarizing, interpreting, and communicating financial information. It reveals profit or loss for a given period, and the value and nature of a firm's assets, liabilities, and owners' equity. Accounting provides information on the resources available to a firm, the means employed to finance those resources, and the results achieved through their use."

If you are not good with accounting, or not using your accounting software regularly, you should hire a professional accountant. There are three levels of accounting experts you can hire to help you: a bookkeeper, an accountant, and a certified public accountant, or CPA. The main differences between these providers are their hourly rates and their level of expertise, and some don't do taxes.

A Bookkeeper records your receipts and expenses in accounting software either weekly or monthly. They are typically an outsourced vendor to your small business. Bookkeepers are primarily accounting clerks responsible for recording accounting transactions and reconciling your bank statements. They will set up your accounting software and enter data regularly and print your monthly financial statements. Their focus is your monthly reconciliation. Bookkeepers do not typically do business taxes. They also will not advise you on tax planning. What they can do is teach you how to read and understand your monthly financial statements and develop a budget for your business.

An Accountant is someone who might work as an employee of your company or as a contractor. They are qualified to handle the day-to-day bookkeeping needs of a small business. They manage accounts payable and accounts receivable and data entry into your accounting system. They provide management, budgeting, and analysis of your financial records. They also handle payroll, and some do business taxes. Accountants generally have college degrees and are trained to interpret financial data. They have a higher skill level than bookkeepers.

A Certified Public Accountant (CPA) is a licensed accountant who has passed a rigorous state examination. They can do the full range of accounting services, but many specialize in taxes and audits. Only CPAs can certify an audit. CPA firms will often refer bookkeepers to their customers as they focus on providing business consulting and tax planning services in addition to tax preparation services. They are highly qualified experts in accounting, and as such, are expensive.

When you are hiring an accountant, you want a professional who has experience with small businesses. Your accountant should be easy to talk to and good at explaining terms like depreciation, chart of accounts, cost of goods sold, balance sheets, and other financial terms, which may be new to you. You also need this expert to help you create your pricing model. You may want to consider a smaller accounting firm or a solo practice over a large accounting firm because costs are generally lower. Shop around until you find the right fit and ask other business owners for referrals. You can also check in with the Society of Certified Public Accountants. New tax laws are passed every year, so you need someone doing your taxes who is up-to-date on the latest tax law. Your tax professional may not be the same person who does your monthly reconciliation.

Time to get real about your finances

If your accounting records are currently not up-to-date, it's time to get it together. Collect all your recurring monthly bills and invoices aka your accounts payable, all your outstanding customer invoices or accounts receivable, your bank statements, loan documents, credit card statements, and every receipt or strip of paper related to your business. This step is the hardest, but if you don't do it, none of the other steps will work—at all. Oh, and there's really no outsourcing this. Only you know where those old invoices are buried, where that shoebox of receipts are, and how long it's been since you filed taxes. It's also not a bad thing to look at your personal bank statements, pull a credit report, and your current credit score, too. Take a deep breath and get in there and get this done. Once all the records are pulled together you'll be in a position to get some help.

Getting Accounting Help

Grab your EIN number, your incorporation papers, customer lists, payroll statements, and all banking and business paperwork I asked you to collect and find a seasoned bookkeeper to sort through the madness that is your business financial records right now. Even if you consider yourself fairly organized, bookkeepers are hardwired to restructure, reorganize, and detail any missing links, items, or reports. Bookkeepers are true lifesavers for overwhelmed business owners. They can set up your accounting software, create your chart of accounts and input your data, and reconcile your bank records, so you can finally understand what is going on financially in your business.

Once your records are up-to-date, you need to make sure your accounting gets done monthly going forward. You should have financial statements to review by the 15th of each month so that you can make any adjustments to your business operations or start making collection calls. The three financial statements you should review include the balance sheet, cash flow statement, and an income or profit and loss statement.

The Balance Sheet is a statement that shows the business's financial position at a specific moment in time. It highlights assets, liabilities, and capital over a month or a year. **The Cash Flow Statement** shows the sources and uses of cash from one month to the other. You use this to evaluate your cash position in your business. **The Income or Profit and Loss Statement** (P&L) is a statement which shows sales, direct costs, expenses, and profit over a period of time, such as a month or a year.

Hire a Tax Professional

Once you are armed with up-to-date financial records, you should hire an accountant or CPA as a business advisor to discuss the financial health of your business. You should also have this expert file any delinquent tax returns, filing extensions, or figure out what you owe in current quarterly taxes. You also need to decide who will do your monthly accounting on an ongoing basis. You might want to keep using the seasoned bookkeeper that helped you pull everything together initially, or you may want your tax accountant to handle everything. You just need to get a process in place so that you can focus on your most high-valued activities like bringing in more sales. Remember, you need up-to-date financial information to run your business better. It's important to track your business growth (or lack thereof) and profitability year over year.

Your Business Plan

Without a solid business plan, you'll be missing the basis for many financial decisions. Your business plan should include an executive summary, clear business goals, demonstration of your knowledge of the market and your opportunity, detailed product or service descriptions, target customer profile, a marketing plan, an operations plan, and realistic financial projections including a 12-month cash flow statement. Your business plan can also help you resist wasteful spending opportunities.

Maybe you started out with a business plan when you first started your business, but now it's on a shelf or in a drawer or lost on your hard drive somewhere. If so, find it, read it, and evaluate it. Does it still work? Do your assumptions still make sense based on your historical knowledge of your business or is your first business plan laughable? Is your target audience who you thought it would be? If not, put updating your business plan on your list of things to fix. By the way, I offer a six-week online course on how to write a business plan, which is designed for existing business owners in case you need some help. Get more details at FixYourBusiness.com.

We'll deal with your company's 3- to 5-year plan in Chapter 11, but for now just consider the current short-term and long-term goals for operating a growing business. This will translate into financial needs and be supported by your financial decisions. Unless your business plan and finances are integrated, you can't manage your money effectively.

Budgeting and Accounting Software

One of the most important things you need in your business is a budget. You need a breakdown of how much money you have, how much you need to spend, and how much you need to bring in to meet your business sales goals. Before you can make money, you must figure out how to spend it. Drafting a budget is a key way to help you turn your business dream into reality. Using accounting software, you can track cash on hand, business expenses, and how much revenue you need to keep your business going every month. You can also use this information to understand your break-even points and track the profitability of every deal.

If you take the time to develop a budget, you are far more likely to utilize it to anticipate future cash needs, project spending, and track your profit. It also may let you spot budget challenges before they pop up. This will position you to borrow money before you need it, if possible. You should also share the budget with your employees, so that they understand the cash needs of the business and stay focused on monthly sales goals. Hopefully it will motivate them to work harder.

Watch Your Spending

One of the easiest ways to make your business more profitable is to curtail your spending. You should consult your budget before making purchasing decisions or deciding to invest in new marketing initiatives. Also ask yourself "why?" three times—and get three different answers—before making any major purchase decisions for your business.

Your accountant or bookkeeper can help you decide which accounting software to use. You want to pick software that can meet the needs of your business for the next few years, not just where you are today. Make sure you use a cloud-based option, so that you can access your records online or fire off an invoice from a mobile device. The software you choose depends on your business, how you get paid, and how may transactions you handle monthly. Do you handle hundreds of transactions at cash registers or online every day? Or do you send a few invoices to several customers who pay by check or wire transfer? Do you handle payroll or outsource it? Do you have affiliates or multiple salespeople whose revenue you need to track? There are several good cloud-based accounting software programs available. Head over to FixYourBusiness.com for my best accounting resources.

Business transactions move at a faster pace than ever given advances in technology, so you must be ready to make decisions quickly. You should make business decisions based on current and accurate financial data. Use your Profit and Loss Statement (P&L) to give you a comparative look at where money is coming in from and where you are spending it. You also need accurate financial statements when you are ready to pursue a bank loan or alternative financing, as I'll discuss a bit later.

A QUICK FIX
FINANCIAL FORMS, REPORTS, TEMPLATES

1. Accounting software comes with tools, templates, and forms to keep track of financial transactions, for invoicing and check printing, and to project future needs.

2. When you need to build a budget, leverage your software for historical data or have your accountant help you.

3. When building sales projections, start with the expenses in your spreadsheet then you'll have an idea of the sales needed to run the business.

4. Use time tracking and employee scheduling software to track, manage, report, and bill time.

5. Sign up for online banking and bill pay to connect your accounting software to your bank account and business credit cards.

Create a One-Year Budget for Your Business

We've already established the need for an annual budget, but if you created one, when was the last time you looked at it? As circumstances change, you must revise your budget to align with current receivables, payables, and expenses. It's best to evaluate your budget line-by-line on a quarterly basis. Also, if you don't review how your business is performing year to year, you won't know how to improve performance, where to make cuts, or whether you have the available funds to purchase new equipment such as computers, delivery trucks, or ERP software. You need information to improve cash flow management so you don't find yourself in fiscal trouble and stressed out.

Your budget will tell you the hard, cold truth about your business. But once you have it in hand, I promise you'll feel more in control, which leads to less cash flow chaos. Whew!

Get On Top of Your Numbers

Now that you have all your numbers in order, the real work of making the money work for you can begin.

Many small businesses don't last because the business owner doesn't understand the importance of the numbers behind the business. You don't need to be a CPA, but you do have to be willing to examine the numbers honestly and understand the stories they tell.

Manage Your Cash Flow

Cash flow keeps your doors open and the bills paid. It compensates you, your employees and vendors, lets you upgrade your equipment, and order supplies and inventory to stock your shelves. When cash flow slows to a trickle, you immediately feel the burn. Poor cash flow can doom even profitable companies. Struggling to collect payments from clients and having invoices that linger for more than 60 to 90 days are shockingly common problems for small business owners. It's almost like the larger the customer the longer it takes them to pay their small business vendors.

Here's a tip though; outstanding customer service is essential to maintain and increase your customers and incentivize them to take care of you. Happy customers are more likely to pay you on time. Offering multiple payment methods (like cash, checks, EFT, Mobile Wallet, credit cards, and PayPal payments) also helps customers to pay faster. This means the stars don't have to be aligned so the customer has money, an envelope, and postage stamps all at the same time.

In my business, I check my business accounts daily, and I focus on managing cash flow weekly so I can keep my stress level down and focus on what I do best—attract customers and build my brand. Here are some of the best ways to manage cash flow in a small business.

Watch for Signs of a Cash Crisis

Think of your cash flow management system as the veins and arteries that deliver blood to different parts of your body. If your blood gets misdirected or suddenly halts, you're in serious trouble. The same is true for cash flow in your business. Even if your customers continue to pump money into your business, unless they do it in a timely manner it often can feel like a blockage to your heart.

One of the biggest signs of a pending cash crisis is if you're consistently spending more money than you bring in. Or if you're spending down your operating capital to exactly when the next check is coming. If you never have cash reserves, something needs to change. Perhaps you need better money rules, accounting procedures, fewer employees, better document management, or more favorable payment terms. Try to negotiate monthly retainer agreements, at least 30% to 50% fees in advance and transfer as many customers as you can to electronic funds payments, which will help you get paid faster. Waiting for a check and then depositing it in the bank will slow down your money flow. Beware of banks that hold big checks for three to five business days. Shop around for a business bank that clears checks overnight.

Consider Going Cashless

If you are a business that handles a lot of transactions daily, such as a restaurant, consider going cashless. There is a cost to handling cash, and you are five times more like to encounter employee theft than a robbery, so why not remove the potential issue? You also want to move people through your checkout line as fast as possible.

People live on their smartphones. Seventy percent of the world—or more than five billion people—will be connected via mobile device by 2020, meaning there will be more users who can make purchases electronically than ever before. The average phone user in the US checks their phone more than 150 times a day. If you are in retail or run a food service business, why not make sure that there's one more way for your customers to do business with you? Going digital allows your patrons to pay via device. Additionally, wouldn't it be great to spend less time reconciling the cash register every night at close?

Going cashless takes the concept of grab-and-go to a whole different level. This is a huge opportunity for your business to meet the growing demand of your customers. As millennials become an increasingly important customer base and more commerce is initiated via mobile device, adding digital payments to the equation makes your business look tech-savvy, and could increase your takeout or delivery business. It's fast, convenient, safe, and future-proof.

Collect Money as Fast as You Can

You want the time it takes you to get paid (days in Accounts Receivable—AR) to be shorter than the time it takes you to pay your obligations (Accounts Payable—AP days). When this is the case, cash flow is generally better, and you can negotiate favorable terms for paying your suppliers. It makes intuitive sense that your business should collect money faster than paying money out, but that's not always under your control.

Whenever you can, negotiate up-front payments, but recognize that some clients won't let you bill until 30 days after you start work. If you get this dynamic backwards too often, problems can become severe enough to threaten your business altogether. Once you are an established business, you'll need to secure a line of credit from a bank to float the business until your invoices are paid. Keep in mind a bank will typically loan your business only 10% of your gross revenue in a line of credit. As a small business owner, you can expect to face occasional cash flow hiccups, but overall, having the AR and AP balance in your favor is a huge advantage.

A Word of Caution About Lines of Credit

Lines of credit are really designed to be used for short-term expenses, such as payroll or inventory to fill an order. As soon as you get the payment you are waiting on you should immediately pay down your line of credit. Try to always start the year with zero balance. Just before the most recent market crash, many small business owners had their lines of credit rescinded or "termed out" into traditional loans. This was especially true for businesses who had only made interest payments. Be sure to make a principal payment at least once a year to stay in compliance with the bank requirements. Also, you will be required to give a personal guarantee for your business line of credit which means you are personally liable for the total value of the loan if the business cannot pay. Banks may place liens against your personal residence as part of these guarantees and this can be done without your knowledge, so just be informed.

Establish Collection Procedures

Don't assume that an invoice automatically translates into a signed check. It doesn't. If your customers or clients accept goods or services on a net-30 or net-60 basis, you must have collection policies in place.

First, send your bills out as soon as possible. If you hear nothing for 30 days, on day 31 send a reminder notice and have someone on your team make a phone call to the accounts payable department to inquire about the status of your payment. If you have on-going problems in this area, consider requiring electronic payments or working with a collection agency. The investment in outsourcing collections can pay off in terms of better cash flow and less stress.

Of course, your collection procedures won't work if your customers don't know what to expect. Before you finalize a contract, put in writing the details of your payment terms. Ask for the name and contact information for the accounts payable department. It's often not your actual customer causing the issue, although you do need to make sure they submitted your invoice in a timely manner to accounts payable. Let your customers know when installment and final payments are due as well as the consequences for missing a deadline, such as interest charges.

I've seen businesses flourish despite low revenue, especially in the beginning, but I've also met entrepreneurs who have declared bankruptcy despite tremendous revenue due to chronic slow-paying clients. Getting on top of cash flow management early and managing your business with a budget offers the solution to this problem.

Mini FIX
TWO INCENTIVES TO PAY

REWARD

Offer a discount for early payment. Decide how much money you're willing to part with in order to get paid on time. Perhaps a 2% discount if the invoice is paid 7 days early, or even 5% off if they pay 14 days early. Make the amount enough to motivate them to pay early.

PENALTY

Charge a penalty for late payments, such as 1.0% or 1.5% per month. Or simply name a higher price if paid after _____ date.

Whichever incentive you decide to offer, announce it in your payment policy. Make it part of your contracts. It's imperative that you clearly communicate any changes to your clients, as well as give them a heads up of at least one billing cycle before a new policy kicks in. Be fair, but be serious.

Consider each on a case-by-case basis. Perhaps one client is having his own financial woes. In that case, set up a payment plan that works for both of you. If it's not a financial problem that's keeping a client from paying on time, consider whether you truly want to continue working with a problematic client like this.

Manage Accounts Payable

Timing your payments strategically is essential to good cash flow management, too. Your goal should be to stretch payables as long as possible without hurting your credit or credibility with your suppliers or contractors. Negotiate net-45 payments with your vendors or a pay-when-paid policy for contractors. Have a set day of the month when you pay vendors.

Explore which vendors offer cash discounts or cash back and whether the deal would be worthwhile. Negotiate favorable credit terms with your suppliers. Life is easier when your cash flow, AR, and AP are all ticking along positively. It's also wise to space out cash disbursements so that you don't have to make a lot of payments right on top of the month.

Let your contractors know that you only cut vendor checks once or twice a month. Be careful with this though. If you wait too long to pay suppliers, you could damage your credit, and they may start demanding prepayment. That would put a huge kink into your cash flow.

Pay your company's bills on time. Be careful to whom you extend credit. Don't ship anything without ink on paper or a purchase order in hand. Pay your bills with a business credit card, but have a strong policy about using it wisely. Use your card to track spending, earn rewards, and dispute charges should there be any issues. Stay away from business credit cards that charge transaction fees and look for cards that charge interest from the billing date rather than the date of purchase. You'll reap benefits from strong cash flow management including lower operating costs, more time to focus on serving customers (because you're not spending time chasing late payments), and better vendor relationships (as you'll be paying them on time). Good cash flow management sets the foundation for fewer average days that accounts spend in AR and for future negotiation of better payment terms with your suppliers.

The Path to Profitability

"Every entrepreneur needs to focus on growing profits for their small business."

Just because you can pencil profit into the financial projections doesn't mean it will automatically come to fruition. As an entrepreneur, commit fully to "minding your own business" to generate the profits that you seek.

Here are several strategies I encourage you to follow as you look to achieve greater profits in your business.

Focus on Profits and Outputs

Constantly evaluate the productivity gains from people and resources. I don't hire someone without knowing the potential return on investment for my business. In other words, I evaluate new hires and contractors by how much revenue they can bring in. As a small business, you can't afford to hire anyone whose work you cannot quantify in billable hours or in work productivity that enables others to achieve more billable hours. Before buying a building, equipment, inventory, or supplies, consider the direct or indirect impact the investment has on your bottom line.

Get Your Hands Dirty

Putting pen to paper and analyzing profit potential doesn't take a lot of painstaking effort. However, putting hands to dirt to execute your plan often does. It is rare to generate profits without hard work. Occasionally, you can fall into an opportunity, but by and large you will fight for most business opportunities, particularly if you operate in the B2B marketplace or as an e-commerce business. The competition is fierce and B2B opportunities can often be political. Always do what you can to reduce costs. Initially small business owners often change light bulbs, do routine plumbing, clean, and perform other laborious tasks, until they realize their time is more profitable doing high value activities like selling the next job. Here's a money rule: Don't ever spend your time, as a business owner, doing $20 per-hour work. Hiring someone to do these things is much more effective.

Look for Efficiency Gains

Look at expenses as dead weight in your journey down the road of a profitable business. Do you really need that office space and overhead or can you work from home and be a spare room tycoon? Can you get along without the Mercedes or can you muddle along with a more modest car for now?

A side note: These slashes are uncomfortable, and they should be. No one really gets what they want without sacrificing, but always remember as small business owners we live how most people won't so we can live how most people can't. Your friends with mid-manager corporate jobs and McMansions live in fear of losing a job daily, and many of them work for corporations who do not value them. They envy you. You call your own shots, and it's a wonderful feeling, isn't it? Belt tightening doesn't have to be permanent. You'll eventually get that S-Class Mercedes Benz you always wanted, and at least four vacations a year, once you have your personal and business finances rolling.

Take one day out of the week as your "frugal day." Ask yourself, "Where can I save money today?" Eat at home, skip your Starbucks run, stay off Amazon, you know what I'm talking about. Be frugal in your business too. Do you need name brand toner for your laser printer or is there a generic brand for a third of the price that you can buy? Could you save money by asking one of your employees to drop off packages on their way home, rather than paying for a pick-up? Could you book business travel on points and save cash?

It will become a reflex once you see how these savings boost your profits and take-home pay. Even if things are generally going well, the key to maximizing profit potential in a small business is to always look for efficiency gains. Saving $100 per month on building expenses, reducing banking fees, or buying more used equipment instead of new equipment could all improve profitability.

Efficiency isn't just about cost reduction. You can also do things better or find ways to get the same or greater value without a lower investment. For example, shop around for banks that don't charge monthly fees or any other hidden fees. You can look for a business credit card that offers rewards or cash back for purchases. You are spending the money anyway, so you should benefit from it.

Increase Revenue

Profits don't just come from controlling costs. In fact, the key to optimized profits usually lies more in your ability to scale your revenue up at a higher ratio than your costs. Training your sales team to generate maximum value from each customer is an effective way to accomplish this. More importantly, emphasizing a quality customer experience that leads to repeat purchases, loyalty, and referrals helps amplify your long-term revenue. Attracting new segments of customers is a common revenue growth strategy as well.

Team FIX
YOU MAKE IT OR BREAK IT TOGETHER

Employees typically overestimate the profit that their employer is earning and underestimate the costs of operating. Here are some ways to help them, help you.

1. Have a Q&A or brown bag lunch about "how we make money." Explain how the team contributes to earning money and keeping expenses down.

2. Have a Suggestion Box for money-earning and money-saving ideas. Find a way to implement and reward great ideas. Involve your team in reviewing the options.

3. Give some serious thought to how open you want to be with your employees about your finances. Read about Open Book Management (www.nceo.org/articles/open-book-management). How does being Open Book fit with your leadership style?

4. Have regular team discussions about company growth and profits and where they fit in to that picture.

5. Give your team cost-cutting metrics to achieve. Example: We need to cut our printing expenses by 15% without losing any customers. How can we do that and by when?

Expand Existing Streams of Income

Every fall, you should review your year-to-date financial history for your business to develop a budget for the next year. You should also develop your sales forecast, too. Even if you have had sporadic sales and more expenses than income, knowing exactly where your money is coming from and where it is going is of the utmost importance to growing your business. Once you have that part down, you can analyze what you did to earn those sales and what the next steps might be to grow your sales.

- Who bought from you, and why?
- Did you enjoy working with your customers? If so, where can you find more of them?
- Can you add new products or services to what you currently offer those customers and increase your contract for the new year?
- Can you drill down and focus on a new niche part of your target audience?

We'll work more on increasing revenue in later chapters. For now, let's look at how to secure money, if and when you need to borrow it.

Your Banking Relationship

Many business owners have a bank, but what you need is a banking relationship. Entrepreneurs with a bank just make deposits and withdrawals. Business owners with a banking relationship know the branch manager, the business banker, and the head teller at the bank they use. The business banker has seen your business plan and is aware of any big contracts or awards that the company has received. The head teller knows you so you can deposit a check as cash based on your reputation, not your balance.

Why is this relationship important? As a business owner, eventually you will need money. Once you have a track record in business with positive activity on your balance sheet, you can consider approaching a bank for a loan. Cultivating a positive relationship with a bank prior to having a need for a loan is really important. It could mean the difference between success and failure. Here are some points to consider:

- **Look local**. Look first for a local bank or Community Development Financial Institution (CDFI) that can address your needs. Look for institutions that focus on providing loans in the community or to small businesses. Visit the lender in person from time to time so people know your face. Use these visits to keep senior personnel up to date on your business activities. CDFIs are a great option if you are turned down for a loan from a traditional bank. Go to FixYourBusiness.com for a list of CDFI lenders in your state.

- **Do your homework.** Know your credit history before you go for a business loan or line of credit. It is essential to keep your credit score as high as possible. Banks will only make loans to clients with good credit. Even a CDFI will not work with you to secure a loan if your personal credit score is below 640.

- **Be prepared.** You'll need a few things to apply for a business loan including a current business plan, two years of personal and business taxes, business bank statements, a current P&L statement, and a strategy for repayment. When applying for a business loan, remember that 90% of the decision is based on two things: your cash flow and your current net worth. The remaining 10% of the decision is based on your credit history and your business viability.

Timing is everything when it comes to borrowing money. If you wait until you're underwater to apply, most banks will politely usher you out the door, plus they don't move that fast. It could take two to three months to get a bank loan. It's best to borrow money when you're financially healthy, as in when you don't need it, to be successful.

Keep in mind that credit unions and nonprofits may also offer small business loans. These organizations may give smaller loans than banks, but they are often a great first step in securing financing and establishing business credit. Find your local Small Business Development Center (SBDC) or other small business nonprofits that have a micro-lending program. Such groups often have loan packaging deals under $50,000 and more importantly, many have special relationships with financial institutions that will work hard to approve clients with less than stellar credit.

Alternative Lenders

Eight thousand small business loans are turned down per day in the US, and this has created an amazing industry of alternative funders and cash advance lenders. This is expensive money, but sometimes desperate times call for the need to borrow funds just to keep your business going. There are plenty of lenders willing to do these unsecured cash advance loans, but there's a hefty interest rate to pay. There's also peer lending, crowd-funding, and factoring, too. Here's the skinny on alternative lending options.

Peer-to-Peer Lending Networks

One alternative funding option is a peer-to-peer lending network. These networks allow lending transactions to take place directly between individuals. If you want to use this option, you can use online companies such as KIVA.org or LendingClub.com. On these sites, business owners request a specific amount (from $50 to $25,000) at a specific interest rate, and lenders fund all or portions of the loan. Lenders are then paid back with interest over a specific time frame.

Crowdfunding

Raising money via crowdfunding is another way for small businesses to build capital for a new or growing venture, but it's a lot of work. Crowdfunding success comes down to your story, your cause or mission, how cool and useful your product is, and your marketing campaign. It's almost like running another business, and the average campaign raises roughly $10,000—one might argue that it's as much a marketing tool as it is a financial tool. Many product-based businesses have used crowdfunding campaigns to build customer base and secure capital to mass produce their product, but the most successful campaigns have resources to produce a compelling video, build an effective e-mail marketing campaign, and provide enticing rewards. If you have the time to plan a successful strategy, your crowdfunding campaign could launch into a million-dollar brand or be a big distraction to you running your business.

Factoring

Factoring is a financing method in which a business owner sells invoices or accounts receivable at a discount to a third-party funding source to raise capital. Business factors can get up to 95% of the face value of your invoices in cash within 24-48 hours.

Cash Advance Loans

If your business has positive cash flow, and you have decent credit, you can get an unsecured cash advance business loan. You'll need to provide at least six months of bank statements and your most recent business taxes, but no collateral is required. You could be charged on the low end a 16.99% interest rate all the way up to as high as a 65% interest rate on a 6- to 12-month loan. So, if you need a $40,000 loan, and you have good credit in the 740s, you could get a loan where the repayment is $51,863.00, roughly 32% interest on a 12-month loan. Your payments will be deducted from your bank account daily or weekly, depending on your business transaction rate, and in some cases, all the interest is factored in on the loan up front, so there's no real discount to paying it off early. One advantage of these loans is the speed with which they can happen. Often you can have the money wired to your bank account in no more than days.

Regardless of the type of funding option you pursue, there are nine questions every small business owner needs to answer before applying for any loan.

Personal FIX

Nine questions to ask yourself before pursuing funding for your business

1. What are the biggest challenges confronting your business?

Be honest with yourself about whether or not money is really going to solve the problems in your business. Often you might need to fix something else before taking on this kind of expensive capital. Your revenue model must be tight.

2. What is really working well in your business that can spur your growth?

Are you selling out of inventory quickly? Do you have customers lined up, but you just need capital to order materials/equipment to do the work? You want to make sure that you have a way to turn this cash into more cash quickly and repay your loan. Alternative funding is for businesses with immediate working capital needs, it's not smart to use these funds for long-term investments such as marketing.

3. How much capital are you looking for?

You need to have a clear idea of how much money you really need. Often people guess at these numbers. Sit down with your accountant and work through what is really needed to grow your business. Then ask for 10% more than the minimum needed. Keep in mind that you must be realistic. No one will loan you more than 10% to 15% of your gross revenue unless you have a signed contract or invoices to sell.

4. What will the capital be used for?

Once you know how much money you need, write up a Strategic Plan for what you are going to do with the cash. Be as specific as possible. Also, highlight how much money this cash will make the business. You want to make sure that your sales are enough to make a healthy profit to pay back the loan, otherwise it might not be worth taking the money.

5. Have you already sought conventional bank financing?

Always try the bank first. Conventional bank money is much cheaper than alternative lenders, but it's also really hard to get, especially when you really need it. You want to apply for a bank loan or line of credit when times are good, not when you are going through a hardship situation. Banks also don't move fast. Remember, your personal credit will play a role in any lending decision someone makes about your business.

6. What is your expected return on the capital requested?

You want to insure the return on investment EXCEEDS the cost of the capital. Develop a clear plan for how many times you can turn the money over in your business.

7. Do you understand the cost of this capital?

In some cases, you could be charged on the low end *16.99%* interest all the way up to as high as *65%* interest on a 6- to 12-month loan. These loans rarely are extended more than a year.

8. How will your payments be collected?

Typically, your payments will be deducted from your bank account daily, weekly, or monthly as an auto draft from your checking account.

9. Are there any closing costs or penalties for early payoff with this alternative loan?

Often lenders and brokers will add fees to these cash advance loans of $2,000 to $5,000 depending on the size of the loan. The money is deducted off the top of the loan. Also ask about any penalties for an early payoff.

Expert Interview

Keeping Profit First in Your Small Business
*Candid interview with small business expert and
author Mike Michalowicz*

You've run many businesses over the years; staying on top of your numbers became your secret weapon. How did you do it?

So, in the beginning I didn't stay on top of my numbers. I lived in that daily stress of check-to-check living, not having enough revenue coming into my business at times and going into a panic "sell anything to anybody" mode. Other times getting tons of money and thinking I had the money to spend on expenses, but didn't address my own compensation. Basically, I paid out all the money that came into the business before I would pay myself.

About 10 years ago, I implemented the Profit First system for myself. I knew I couldn't do what my accountant was telling me to do—he was telling me to read and live off of the accounting statements. But the reality is I ignored those statements and just would look at my bank balance. So, with Profit First, I run my entire business off of my bank accounts. But instead of having just one checking out, I now have many accounts that act like envelopes for money. Each account has a specific purpose, and when money comes in, I first allocate money to each account before ever spending it. I know exactly what money is allocated to what purpose before I spend a dime. And that's become my secret weapon.

You are a big advocate of small businesses having a profit account. What is that?

The profit account is the foundational component of Profit First. It is a dedicated savings or checking account where you allocate a percentage of your income to profit before you do anything else. Yes, you take a pre-determined percentage, be it 5% or 10 or 20%, or whatever. Every time a deposit comes in, you transfer that percentage of money into the profit account and then work with the rest. But you must be focused to do this. To start building a profit account, you need to remove your profit income before you even have access to it and "hide" it from yourself. That's why I call the system Profit First and that's the money that the profit account stores. I would suggest using the Profit First system, and then use your Income Statement to discover what is making you money (and do more of that) and what is costing you money (like unnecessary expenses, and remove them).

So how do you get started building a Profit First account?
Start taking a profit. Now this is big if you've never been profitable. I don't suggest starting at 50% of income for profit—that's too abrupt of a change. Instead, start by taking a very small percentage; probably just 1% to start. Then after a quarter (90 days) take 2% and 3% to grow that profit percentage. Always start small. Never rewind and never take 10% and say "oh it is not working now" and take 5%. We're not going to get momentum that way. So, start small and continue to take small steps toward more profit. Be relentless. Always take the profit first.

What strategies can business owners use to better manage their finances?
Business owners need to also remove temptation from "borrowing" their profit money. And I'm doing air quotes when I say "borrow" since business owners will steal from themselves. They have bills that are piling up and can't pay them, so they take from their profit account to pay the bills. This wipes out their profit and defeats the entire system. You need to remember a critical lesson: If you can't pay your bills, that is your business telling you that you can't afford your bills. Perhaps it's time to look at your revenue model.

How can a business owner increase revenue and grow profits?
The process is simple for any business that wants to increase revenue and grow profits. The business owner must concentrate on selling the products or services that are generating the biggest profit and identify how and where he/she can increase margins. Remove or change the things that are not profitable, extract more value out of employees and investments, and always cut unnecessary costs.

Your book, *Pumpkin Plan*, is one of my favorites. Can you briefly explain the connection between seed selection and higher profit margins?
The idea of better seed selection is to position your business for optimal growth. Similar to planting a pumpkin for colossal growth, you need to pick a seed that best matches the environment. With your business, the optimal seed is where you plan your business around serving your best customers even better, deliver a product/service that is so unique they can't get the same elsewhere, and you systematize your business to a degree that it can grow independently. I have found that most businesses only get one or two of these components done right. To achieve higher profit margins, you need to get all three right. It is that simple.

What is your best advice for business owners who are reinventing their businesses?
Don't pivot. Align.

In an attempt to reinvent their business, most owners try to pivot to their customers' needs, which means they change their offering to meet what the customer needs. But the problem is, I have seen countless businesses pivot right out of their passion. Meaning, business owners find ways to stay afloat making money, but they fall out of love with their business. Instead of pivoting, business owners must constantly align. We must identify what our customers want and need, and at the same time, we must make sure it is within our field of passion.

About the Expert:

Mike Michalowicz is the entrepreneur behind three multi-million dollar companies and is the author of *Profit First*, *The Pumpkin Plan*, and the entrepreneur's cult classic, *The Toilet Paper Entrepreneur*. Mike is a former small business columnist for *The Wall Street Journal*, and regularly travels the globe as an entrepreneurial advocate. Learn more at www.MikeMichalowicz.com.

FIX YOUR PROFIT

**EMERSON'S URGENCIES:
SEEK HELP IMMEDIATELY!**

If you are about to default on a business loan, file for bankruptcy, or lose your business for financial reasons, you need a plan. And you need professional help. What steps can you take immediately to get the help you need?
1.
2.
3.

How well do you understand your business's finances? Are your taxes up-to-date? If you really don't know your numbers, make a plan for how to learn and how to outsource this to get some help. Here are some steps to take. Feel free to add your own, and then put them in order.

1. Ask my kitchen cabinet for help.
2. How should I get this under control?
3. Do I have a friend or adviser who is knowledgeable about finances?
4. When am I going to pull all my records together?
5. Figure out the costs of learning to do it myself vs. outsourcing accounting.
6. Figure out what kind of accounting professional I need, and how often?
7. Hire a seasoned bookkeeper.
8. Make a timeline for what must happen and by when?

Is there one financial issue that is limiting your growth? Brainstorm the issues below.
(We'll work on this more in your Strategic Plan in Chapter 11.)

FIX YOUR BUSINESS ACTION STEPS

For each of these items discussed in Chapter 4: Profit, decide where it falls in your priority action list for a FIX. Add any additional items to the list as needed:

1 = it needs immediate attention, highest priority
2 = it needs a FIX within my 90-day plan, get started now
3 = it can wait, save it for my Strategic Plan in Chapter 11
4 = I have this under control; it doesn't need fixing

TOPIC	1	2	3	4
Business Plan				
Budget				
Taxes				
Bookkeeping				
Banking				
Cash Flow				
Spending				
Revenue				
Profit Margin				
Pricing				

CHAPTER 5: PROCESSES
BUILD SYSTEMS TO DELEGATE AND SCALE

Building processes and systems is all about creating time freedom for the business owner and building scalability. You'll never be able to hire help if you can't explain how things need to get done. As a reformed workaholic, I know how hard it is to delegate significant tasks to others, but I promised you that I was going to reduce chaos in your business, and getting your processes documented is key to that happening. Once you really understand how things get done, you can unplug from your business more. And your employees, family, and all your personal relationships need you to have an opportunity to recharge and think about something other than your business from time to time.

If you are a Type A control freak like me, I'm sure you find it especially hard to let go, but I will offer you an incentive: nothing will add more intrinsic value to your business than scalable, proprietary processes. You need to document your processes for the simple reason that you can't delegate even the simplest tasks without them. You also need to be able to teach "your signature way" of doing things to your team—from how your business operates, to how you earn revenue, and how you engage with clients.

Process Means Profit

In order for your team to learn to do those things really well, you have to document all the processes by which you deliver great service and produce exceptional products. This, in turn, will make your company worth more money than just what you earn every year. With properly documented processes and systems, the possibilities are endless for what you can do with your business.

- You could grow your company to a much, much larger operation, serving many more customers and making far bigger profits.
- You could turn it into a franchise operation and replicate it all over the country or the world.
- Or you could sell it to another entrepreneur or corporation that wants to incorporate your processes into a bigger enterprise. You will have options once you tighten up how your business operates.

A process is a procedure, a method, a system, or a way of doing things. It can have different labels in different fields, like consulting, where the strategy area might be called a practice; or for example in golf, where putting could be designated a technique. If you invent a new, previously unknown process, you can seek a patent from the government, which if issued, would legally prevent anyone else from copying your process for fourteen to twenty years.

If you are in the business of making things—anything from craft items to complex manufactured goods, like software to age-defying sunscreen to specialty doughnuts, you must keep working on the processes (formula, recipe, design) that create the products and the systems in your business to produce and execute them.

Typically, you start to produce items in small quantities by yourself or with a friend helping you to create a minimal viable product and test the marketplace; next it will evolve into a professional prototype that you can use for mass production. Your processes become priceless assets to your business, unless you fail to protect them from the beginning. It's time to look at this Pre FIX.

Pre FIX
Protecting Your Business Assets

Do You Have a Proper Legal Entity?
Setting up a legal entity such as an S-Corp or LLC is a common way to establish and protect a business. It's an important step in the development of your business and protection of your valuable business assets. It's not enough just to incorporate your business, there are record requirements such an annual meetings and meeting minutes that must be maintained. You also need to maintain a separate bank account and checkbook for your business, and use the company name on all documents.

Use Proper Contracts and Follow the Law
One of the easiest ways for a business to be vulnerable to someone stealing your business assets is if you act negligently or fraudulently. This can be avoided by having good contracts, non-compete/non-disclosure agreements, and written employment contracts for your vendors, manufacturing partners, subcontractors, and employees. And never hire people to work under the table or classify a worker as an independent contractor who should be a W2 employee. These workers can report your business to the Department of Labor for an employment law violation.

Register Your Business Name
Registering your business name involves registering a "Doing Business As" (DBA) name or trade name. This process shouldn't be confused with incorporation and it

doesn't provide trademark protection. Registering your "Doing Business As" name is simply the process of letting your state government know that you are doing business as a name other than your personal name or the legal name of your LLC or corporation.

Apply for Trademark Protection

If you create a signature process and name it, you may need trademark protection. A trademark protects words, names, symbols, and logos that distinguish goods and services. The name of your signature process is one of your most valuable business assets, so it's worth protecting. You can file for a trademark for less than $300.

File for a Patent

If you invented something or a signature process, you need to protect it by filing a patent application with the US Patent and Trademark Office (PTO). This government agency is responsible for examining patent applications and awarding patents. A patent gives the holder the right to keep others from manufacturing, selling, using, or importing into the United States something similar to what you've invented, for a certain amount of time. But filing a patent application is a complex and expensive legal process, one that costs significant money and takes an average of two years to receive a patent. DIY is not recommended here. You'll need a patent attorney or an inventor's association such as Invent.org to help you.

To process is also a verb, meaning to handle, manage, deal with, or sort out, as in "Let's process these orders before we leave." As you work through this chapter and beyond to build your next-level business, you and your team will be "processing" a lot of information and refining exactly how things get done in your business. Along the way, I am sure you'll find some places where processes can be improved!

Some people resist documenting "processes," just as some folks resist "project management," because it seems to them that developing formal "processes" makes things very complicated. Maybe they've seen flow charts or process diagrams that they don't understand, and the complexity frightens them. Writing down a process and all its steps in a flow chart is just like defining all the elements of a project in project management software. It is the first step in making a project manageable. Sometimes things are complex, but writing things down makes it easier to accomplish, not harder. So, don't be conned by employees who resist you on this! And if you, yourself, are the resister, get yourself an accountability coach and get over it. This work must be done! Often, complex things are not easy to deal with in business, but they are totally worth it when you get the results you desire.

Start with Workflow Processes

It is critical that you track workflow in your business. It keeps your company's success, quality control, and productivity uniform. But whether you are just starting to document your business processes, or taking your processes to the next level, plan this project in a way that allows you to manage the work you do efficiently. You and your team will be taking down the rough draft of steps in your simpler processes—those that document the basics of each person's daily activities. Keep in mind that for some jobs you could have a non-reader or a bad speller or a second language speaker, and you don't want to put anyone in an embarrassing spot. Make it clear to everyone that they can write out their job tasks or speak them into a smartphone or audio device.

A side note: If you know or if you discover you have employees with language needs, quietly provide them with the opportunity for formal instruction at your expense. If you have a bilingual workforce, provide instruction in both languages to everyone. You will always be an employer of choice for making this investment in your team!

Okay, once you have the tasks identified and the steps written down, you'll want to put them in a uniform format and have a place to keep them. I recommend that each employee keep their processes updated quarterly online in a public folder that anyone on the team can access. Keep your entire task library online using Google Docs or in project management software. That way should any key employee have unexpected time off due to illness, a family emergency, or suddenly quit, your business can keep moving forward and not be held hostage trying to get information from someone who is no longer available.

It's important to make all your processes look professional, neat, and consistent with your brand identity.

- Do you have a brand style guide for your business?
- Do you have an admin or a virtual assistant with the skills to develop this guide?
- Do you have an employee with the proper skills and time to do this?
- If not, look for a freelancer from Fiverr.com or Upwork.com for a job like this. Try them out with a small assignment first.

Once you've figured out what the end document will look like, and where it will be stored, start sketching out your workflows that need to be tracked. Estimate the time it will take, who will be involved, when you want to get started, and the deadline for completion. If you haven't started documenting your business processes, here are some tips to get everyone fully engaged.

1. **Get the team together**. In a team meeting, explain your goal of documenting your business processes. Let them know why this is important to the business and how you expect them to be involved. Sometimes employees fear that documenting just how they do things makes them vulnerable to being replaced by someone junior to them—someone less experienced and therefore cheaper.

As the leader, it's your job to help them know that the company strength comes from shared knowledge and cross training. They will each be more valuable knowing how to cover for one another and getting ideas for how to improve processes to make them faster (to save money) or better (to improve customer service, product quality, or service delivery). Also, be sure to point out that once these processes generate more profit, that will mean better pay, added benefits, and possibly bonuses. Use whatever you need to so you can paint your big picture for your team to dig in and do this work. They need to see their role in your company's future. You can also set little goals and rewards along the way of the "processes project." Start with Daily Tasks, then move to Weekly Checklists, and later into pick apart the Signature Processes.

2. **Have your employees write down their daily tasks.** Do this for a week, and then work with them to make categories of tasks that occur daily, weekly, monthly, quarterly, and yearly. Ask them to write down things such as:

   - How do they learn their work schedule?
   - How often do they check the PO Box or voice mail?
   - How do they handle customer inquiries?
   - What daily or weekly sales activities are done?
   - To whom do they hand-off documents or products for approvals & quality checks?
   - What services do they perform for your customers?
   - What tasks do they perform with other employees?
   - Where do they keep things such as invoices, contracts, and petty cash receipts?
   - How often do they turn in time sheets? To whom?
   - How and where do they order supplies?
   - How do they get permission to do things—for a day off, a vacation, to purchase something they need for the business, etc.?
   - How do they report a problem or error?

Team FIX
SHOW SOME PROCESS DIAGRAMS

Use to show a progression or sequential steps in a task, process, or workflow, or to emphasize movement or direction.

One

Two

Three

Use to show an ascending series of steps or lists of information.

Visit FixYourBusiness.com for more process diagram examples.

3. **Track your own daily activities.** You probably have no idea all the things you do in a day or week. Start tracking your own activities for a week. Make categories of tasks that need to occur daily, weekly, monthly, quarterly, and yearly. And you should also take note of things you need to stop doing.

Remember my money rule about not doing $20/per hour work. Think through stuff like:

- What is your daily routine? Do you have one or are you all over the place?
- What are the tasks that only you can do?
- How do you keep your pipeline filled?
- How do you help service clients?
- How do proposals get done?
- How do you manage your calendar?
- How does paper get on and off your desk?
- When do you cut checks and pay vendors?
- How are expense reports handled?
- When do you review financial statements?
- How is payroll handled?
- How often do you communicate with your team, accountant, lawyer, HR consultant?

Review the task activities that you and the team have prepared. Determine which ones are ready to become simple processes for the respective jobs.

CHECKPOINT

Employee Activities:

Review activities with each team member. Do you agree that each task is part of their job description as you intend it to be? If not, make changes now! Ask your employees which tasks they have mastered, which tasks work fine, and which ones are problematic and need improvement. They might need more training or maybe there's not enough time in their day to complete a task, or the task sequence is not well defined so no one is handling it. Or perhaps the task crosses into another employee's job and no one knows who should handle the task. Make a list of the tasks. Make three columns, "Mastered," "Gets done," "Needs improvement," and then let your team check the appropriate box for how the task gets handled. Then for all mastered tasks, let your employees draft each into a step-by-step process to be returned to you.

For the tasks in the other two categories, if the task is part of the individual employee's job, and she needs help in better defining it, work with her or assign someone to help her clarify how to execute the task and then document it. If it's a poorly defined task, and it's entirely hers, ask her for ideas on how to improve it or allow the team to brainstorm ideas if she doesn't have any. Be sure each task is labeled with the employee's name and date. For tasks that need improvement or otherwise go undone at times because no one person owns them, keep them in a separate list to deal with later.

Your Activities:

Review all your routinely scheduled tasks plus any that you do whenever a ball gets dropped, something is super urgent, or you have an emergency.

1. **Gather all the tasks that you most dislike or that you are very bad at doing**—these are typically things you put off because you are just barely competent or even incompetent at those tasks, and they take you twice as long as they should to execute.

2. **Make a list of any tasks that you could delegate** (if you had enough help and enough money)—that is, you could hire more employees or you could outsource the work. (If you're not sure it can be delegated, put it on your list to find out.)

   Here's an example: are you the one who scoops up dog poop from your lawn before you mow the lawn? You know you can hire out the lawn mowing, but maybe you don't know you can hire out the poop-scooping too!

3. **Prioritize your list, with #1 tasks you can delegate.** Start with all the tasks that you can delegate right away to an existing employee, an assistant, a child (yes, if kids like money

they should work for it), or find an outsource solution that you can afford (see Chapter 3: People).

4. **Continue to prioritize your list, with #2 tasks that you will delegate as soon as it is possible.** Discuss this list with your kitchen cabinet and make it part of your Strategic Plan in Chapter 11.

Personal FIX
WHAT'S YOUR MARKET VALUE?

Small business owners tend to undervalue their own time on an hourly basis. Just for fun, check out the local going rate for these professionals, and make sure you value your own time at least on par:

1. Law Firm Partner _____ per hour

2. CPA or Practice Manager _____ per hour

3. Management Consultant, Owner _____ per hour

Add some services you use, and be sure you're always earning more than you have to pay:

4. _____ _____ per hour

5. _____ _____ per hour

6. _____ _____ per hour

MORE PLANNING STEPS

Develop checklists. Checklists enable multiple people who are performing the same task to do it in a consistent way and keep your brand promise. A checklist prevents memory loss. When things need to be done in a specific order, you need a process. But when you need to know what kind of clothes to pack, what toiletries to bring, what shoes to pack, etc., a checklist will do the trick. Developing a checklist is a good exercise for you as a business owner, too. Getting the task list out of your head will enable you to hire a virtual assistant or admin to help you run your life and your business. Start with an outline of items, then add more detail as needed.

Examples of checklists for a business include:

- The owner's travel checklist
- Trade show exhibit booth checklist
- Kitchen cleaning checklist
- Product shipping checklist
- Conference staff/supplies checklist
- Sales meeting checklist

Design internal processes. Now it's time to get serious. Your business will never scale unless you have good internal processes. You can have the best services and products, but if your workflow or back office is not in order as your business grows, you will make many expensive mistakes and your customers will not have a consistent experience, which will kill opportunities for repeat business. It will also be nearly impossible to delegate and bring on new employees. As a business owner, your goal should be to figure out how to make money without every dollar touching one of your two hands.

You should aim to future-proof your internal processes, so they can scale with your sales growth. Eventually, this will become the company playbook, and it will free you to go on vacation and sleep well knowing everything is running as if you are there.

Here's my recommendation for how to scope out all the processes that you might need to develop for your business. Go through my list of *The 12 Ps of Running a Successful Business* and see what processes each word suggests to you. I've given you some starter ideas here:

P-Words	Possible Processes To Be Developed
Preparation	Process What Works Well and What Needs Work in the Business Operations Process for When You Take Vacation Risk Management Processes Disaster Recovery
Purpose	Your Leadership Development Processes Staying Connected to Vision and Mission
People	Your Management Processes Hiring Processes Onboarding Processes Performance Review Processes
Profits	Accounting Processes Monthly Bookkeeping Taxes
Processes	Process Catalog (a list of all your processes!) Opening and Closing the Business Security
Productivity	Technology Processes Communication Document Management Processes E-mail Management Data Management—Customer Data, Inventory, Assets
Performance	Customer Service Delivery Process Exchange/Return Processes Customer Service Training
Product	How to Make Your Products Outsourcing Processes Shipping, Handling, Ordering, Receiving New Product Development
Prospects	Sales Process New Customer Onboarding Business Development Process Customer Relationship Management

Presence	Marketing Processes Content Development Lead Generation Processes Social Media Processes
Planning	SWOT Process Budgeting Process Strategic Planning Process
Perseverance	Annual Processes (Inventory, Clean-Up) Capital Improvements (Equipment, Software, Delivery Trucks, etc.)

As you've worked through the first four chapters, you may have identified some processes to develop, especially in Chapter 3: People, and Chapter 4: Profit. Review your work in those chapters for ideas. You'll be confronted with more as you go through the upcoming chapters, so come back to this chapter as needed to complete your process inventory. Technology tools provide a way to manage many of the processes that you've identified: accounting, social media, CRM, etc. I'm going to deal with those choices in the next chapter. But I'll tell you now, you're better off knowing what kind of processes you need and want before you settle on your technology in many cases.

Where Do Complaints Come From

Finding what's broken is another great way to identify business processes that need fixing. What do your customers complain about? How about your employees? You don't like to hear them, but complaints usually mean something is wrong that must be fixed. Even if you hear complaints that seem unfair to you, maybe they give you the chance to improve on a system or product. Smart manufacturers love certain cranky customers who complain that products won't do things that they're not really designed to do. They have a process to get those complaints to product development and give their engineers and designers new ideas! Think of how these complaints led to innovations we use today.

- Why won't this printer scan things?
- How come this bike won't fit in my trunk?
- These surgical knives aren't curved right.
- It broke when I dropped it!
- I was taking pictures underwater and now it's ruined.

If products don't last long enough, if they discolor, if they shrink when washed, you need better materials sourcing or manufacturing or both. If products break before they arrive to the customer, or they don't arrive when they're supposed to, or if the wrong items get sent, you need better order and packaging processes or a more reliable shipping service. If one of your servers is rude, or the food is not hot, or you're always out of the special-of-the-day by 6:30 p.m., you need better management, training, ordering, and kitchen practices. If your business gets online reviews and they are not 99.99% awesome, make sure that you don't have a process problem! Use the feedback as a report card to seek out processes that can be improved and fix them.

Find the Gaps

In London on the Tube, they say "Mind the Gap" (or don't trip on the space between the platform and the train!). Where are the gaps between areas of responsibility or physical spaces in your company?

- Gaps between "virtual" workers and on-site workers.
- Gaps between the office and off-site or traveling employees— (sometimes there can be a disconnect between salespeople and the team that executes and ships products).
- Gaps between retail employees and warehouse employees.
- Gaps between full-time and part-time employees, year-round and seasonal, day shift and evening workers.
- Gaps between marketing and sales, or sales and operations, or operations and customer service. These can sneak up on you as your company grows.

These Gaps are ripe for process-building or process improvement. You also need to be on the lookout for a Gap between you and your employees. Once you start growing your staff, you'll need to hire managers to help you and this will change the culture of your company. Make sure you stay visible and approachable as your business grows.

If you sell intangible products or services, like insurance, training, or consulting, you probably have a different person delivering the service from the one who sold it. And there's probably a time lag between the sale and the service. Do you have a new client onboarding process to fill that gap? How does the paperwork get from one person to the next? In an e-mail? A text? A conversation? A scribbled note? Who's in charge once something is sold? Who will maintain contact with the client? How will things be handled when there's a late payment? When is it late? You must know these things and build processes that support them.

Reviewing Processes

As you and your team build process documents, you should have a way to review them for improvement. One of the things we have done in my business is conduct an after-action review or AAR. We do this after a big launch, client project, or event is completed. We do them within two weeks of the final deliverable while things are still fresh. I first invite anyone on the team to write an e-mail with personal feedback or anything positive or negative shared from the client or an end user. Then we have a meeting to discuss our findings and consider any suggestions. This is just one way to review processes, but there are many others.

Good internal processes should be:

- Efficient
- Documented
- Repeatable
- Automated (See Chapter 6 for technology tools)

An **efficient** process gets the job done without wasting time or money, in a professional and well-organized way. To make a process more efficient, see if it can be streamlined by combining steps or omitting some. Keep it simple. Look at it from the customer's point of view as well as the manager's and the employee's. Don't make it overly stressful or difficult for the person who performs it. That takes efficiency too far and it becomes inefficient!

A **documented** process has a form that can be shared—it's written down or in a visual diagram that others can understand and repeat. It's also stored in a known place and is retrievable on demand by the people who need it. All company processes should also be stored in a location protected from theft and natural disasters. Maintain your written processes electronically, so that whenever a process is updated, the old version is replaced by the new one in all central locations.

A **repeatable** process will give you the same result every time, if it is followed precisely. A recipe is a repeatable process. Many a good cook makes her own family-favorite dishes without anything written down, but no one else can duplicate hers exactly unless she writes it down for you or lets you watch her and write it. They say the recipe for Coke is hidden in a vault!

Some processes are designed to be repeatable by almost anyone who is trained to follow them. Other processes require highly specialized training and skills. Think of the difference between the process of getting a piece of merchandise wrapped and ready for shipment and the process of performing a parallel bar routine. If the merchandise is heavy, the employee must be able to lift a certain amount of weight, and may be required to climb a ladder, and may need to drive a forklift, and so on. So, the process instructions should include any necessary requirements or prerequisites for the person performing the job.

Pre FIX
PROCESS ACCOMMODATIONS

If you employ 15 or more people, you are subject to the Americans with Disabilities Act, which may require you to provide accommodations to a person with a disability who requests such an accommodation.

Even with fewer employees, you may wish to make it possible for a person with a disability to perform a job process that would require some accommodation, such as modifying equipment or providing an interpreter.

You may wish to consider these possibilities as you work on your processes.

Do you have processes that could be modified as well as others that could not?

Establishing Metrics: Delegation and Accountability of Staff

When you delegate a task to someone else, be sure to delegate accountability along with it. This is just as true for an outsource relationship as for a full-time employee or your kids!

Accountability means metrics:

- When is it to be done
- How often
- To what standard—e.g., how good, how many
- How to hand off, and to whom
- How to report

And perhaps also: what are the consequences of failure to comply:

For an employee:

- First time—review your expectations; explain why this is important

- Second time—reprimand; remind of your expectations
- Third time—formal reprimand in personnel file, etc.

For your children:

- Little ones: Put toys in the toy box before bedtime or they will disappear.
- Grade school: If clothes are not in the hamper before supper, you will not be going to karate or dance class.
- Middle school: If your homework isn't done, you will not get any screen time this weekend.

When you outsource payroll services, office cleaning, pest control, or web design, be sure that your agreements and contracts include metrics and due dates: what is the standard of performance, what are the expected milestones, what is your recourse if standards are not met or services are not delivered timely or at all. If you hire a company to remove snow from your customer parking lot, are they required to do it before your office or store opens, within two hours, or the next day? Be certain the contract is clear, and then hold them accountable—even if you only see them twice a year.

Next Level Signature Processes

Henry Ford and his team created one of the most awesome processes of the Industrial Revolution—the assembly line. Instead of all the workers moving around each car, building them one at a time, the Ford team experimented for several years until they had a moving line where each employee had a fixed place and the emerging car was moved along a continuous line:

Dec. 1, 1913, Henry Ford installed the first moving assembly line for the mass production of an entire automobile. His innovation reduced the time it took to build a car from more than 12 hours to two hours and 30 minutes.

That time savings reduced the price of a Ford to fulfill Henry's PURPOSE to build cars inexpensively enough that everybody could have one!

When you create unique processes, strategic processes that simplify the way things work in your business, you are beginning to define what makes your company special. You and your team will figure out ways of doing things that haven't been done before, and some of these will save you a lot of expense or earn you a lot more profit. Like Henry Ford, you may develop Signature processes that define your brand. These will happen over time if you build a process-oriented business culture that includes your entire team.

EXPERT INTERVIEW

Building Better Processes and Systems in a Small Business
*Candid interview with author and process
improvement expert Laura Posey*

You've run a business for many years. When did you start developing processes in your business?
It wasn't until I was at my wit's end about six years into running my company that I started developing processes. At the time, I had a business partner who was always doing things last minute and it drove me nuts. I decided that we needed to implement some systems and timelines so we weren't always behind the eight ball.

When you are getting started building a system, where should you start?
I start with two systems—one that is going to make the biggest impact on client experience and one that is going to make the biggest impact on cash flow. From there, I think it is important to work backwards from the desired end result. Ask yourself the question, "What is the most important result to have?" then "What do I need to do immediately before that?" Keep repeating that question until you get to the beginning. As a simple example:

   i. What is the most important result for me to have?
      Generating $10,000/month

   ii. What do I need to do immediately before that?
      Close 4 clients @ $2,500 each

   iii. What do I need to do immediately before that?
      Have 12 closing appointments

   iv. What do I need to do immediately before that?
      Have 24 prospect appointments

   v. What do I need to do immediately before that?
      Make 240 prospecting calls

vi. What do I need to do immediately before that?
Put 10 calls per day on my calendar

vii. What do I need to do immediately before that?
Pull a list of 240 names in my target market

viii. What do I need to do immediately before that?
Make a list of my target market's ideal traits

How should you document your signature systems for training employees?
It depends on what kind of system it is. For anything that is online, I like to use a video to record the process. For step-by-step systems, I like to use a checklist format, followed by a short description of each step. I'm big on creating templates and checklists that can be used over and over so steps don't get skipped. Everything can be stored in Google Docs or Dropbox for easy access.

There's good marketing automation and too much marketing automation. Can you explain what should be automated and what still needs a human touch?
I like to use a combo of automation with easy ways for clients to engage individually. For example, I'm all for setting up an autoresponder sequence to send out a promotion e-mail. In the e-mail there is always a way to reach out and ask a question. If I refer to a webpage, that page will have a chat box available so clients can interact with a real person, real time. Of course, you want to make sure you're segmenting your list of prospects by demographics and interest so you're only showing people offers they might be interested in. Just blasting out a bunch of generic e-mails to a list is a surefire way to alienate prospects and clients.

There's lots of technology out here to save time and money, but what do you need to consider before investing in new technology?
Of course, the first thing to consider is your budget. Never over-invest in tech if you can help it. Having said that, you need

to make sure you're buying enough technology to take care of your needs in the long run. It can be very time consuming and expensive to change software down the road. I like to make a list of wants and needs for technology. What do I really need the software to do and what would it be nice to have down the road? Being clear about the difference will keep you from overbuying.

You recommend outsourcing to virtual team members. What do you need to have in place before you can delegate a key task?
Having documentation of what you want done is critical. Don't hire anyone to do a task unless you have a process for them to implement. Otherwise, you're setting them, and yourself, up for failure and disappointment. Make a list of your expectations of behavior as well. We do this through defining core values so each team member knows how you expect them to make decisions and treat others.

What is your best advice for a business owner who is reinventing their business model?
I'm a huge fan of having a success plan. Lay out your values and vision for your ideal company and then spend time plotting the course between where you are now and your vision. Include some key metrics and steps for implementing the systems you need to have in place as you grow.

About the Expert:

Laura Posey brings much passion to her work as Chief Instigator of Simple Success Plans. She is a "firecracker" who likes to create and get things done. She is an internationally recognized speaker and consultant. Laura is the author of *How to Plan Your Entire Year on One Sheet Of Paper, Six Secrets of Sales Magnets,* **and the co-author with Jack Canfield of** *Mastering The Art Of Success.* **For more information, go to www.simplesuccessplans.com.**

FIX YOUR PROCESSES

Make a list of the processes that you want to develop. Organize them into the timeline below.
Right Away
Within 90 Days
Add to Strategic Plan with timeline

FIX YOUR BUSINESS ACTION STEPS

These action steps are based on Chapter 5: Processes. Write down your prioritized list of tasks to delegate and your goal dates to delegate them:

Task to Delegate	Date to Be Delegated

What are the three most important processes that could be developed and/or refined in your businesses to become Signature Business Processes?

1.

2.

3.

Be sure to include these in your Strategic Plan (Chapter 11).

CHAPTER 6: PRODUCTIVITY
USE THE RIGHT TOOLS

Simply put, increasing your productivity will increase your profit—it's all about how much meaningful work gets accomplished in a specific time period. Technology tools constantly raise the bar of competition—the wheel, the fish hook, the printing press, cotton gin, airplane, iPod, smartphone, drones, Alexa—who knows what's new since I wrote this book!

Since you have been in business for a few years, I bet you are using a hodgepodge of technology tools for a whole variety of purposes, and your team members may be using a bunch of their own, especially if they work remotely. I doubt that from the beginning you sat down to decide exactly what kind of systems and tools you wanted to have and how you would grow in to them. I know, I didn't! I looked for simple, inexpensive software and apps that would make daily tasks easier or allow me to delegate more or automate them completely. I wasn't very concerned whether my tech tools would get along with each other, my only concern was solving that day's problem. Sound familiar? Now, as a 20-year veteran of running a small business, having made many expensive mistakes, I have wisdom to share on this subject.

Growing Technology with Your Business

As I have watched my consulting business grow, I needed more sophisticated tools to serve my clients, track my results, and report my outcomes, among other things. I do bigger deals with more complicated contracts and invoicing requirements, so my accounting and project management technology needs have increased. More team members, more complex deals, collaboration with other vendors on behalf of my customers, internal project management, and external project management—it's a lot to keep track of for any one business. And all that requires a need for more robust and integrated technology. And hey! I can't just figure out this stuff! I don't have the time, and frankly, I don't know enough. And I don't want to know enough. I have consultants or people on my team who can bring me choices and explain the costs and benefits in a way that makes sense TO ME! Then I need someone to get it installed, train everyone who needs to use it, and put it to work in my business. That's what you need, too. Maybe you're not quite where you can have it all done for you. I'm not all the way there with everything either, but I always balance what I can invest in next that can save time and money—and sometime those are tough decisions. But it's best to think long-term about your technology systems so that you don't have to keep re-doing things.

Decisions, Decisions

The list of decisions you may need to make is pretty long. Start with some overall decisions about your business because these will make your specific technology choices a whole lot easier.

The nature of your business creates certain requirements, and I can't predict those. If you run a farm, a dry cleaner, a manufacturing plant, a restaurant, a warehouse, a delivery service, or a retail store, you have special needs for your physical space, equipment, and technology that differ from accountants, consultants, and web designers, or from electrical contractors or charter schools.

Let's focus on business technology that every business needs for productivity:

1. Office Management
a) Documents

    1) Producing documents

    2) Printing, copying, scanning, faxing

    3) Collaborating on documents

    4) Storing and retrieving documents

    5) Work Flow

b) Project Management and task assignments

    1) Calendar

    2) Meetings

    3) Time tracking

2. Virtual Office, Mobile Access, Virtual Workforce

3. Communications
a) Receptionist

b) Telephone/voice mail

c) Mail

d) E-mail

e) Internal communication and collaboration

f) Communication with customer

g) Website and social media

4. Financial Management

a) Bookkeeping; invoicing, collections

b) Sales—in store, online

c) Payroll and employee benefits

d) Banking—bank accounts and loans

e) Credit card statements

f) Fulfillment; inventory management, shipping

These are basic categories of technology that help every company become productive if they're chosen well and used appropriately.

Bad News, Good News

You used to start with hardware requirements—desktop computers, printers, telephones, and all the associated wiring and installation required. Today, you can set up a virtual office, whether you work together in physical space or not. In theory, all the tasks I've listed can be handled on a smartphone or tablet. In practice, some employees will need a keyboard and a good monitor, maybe two monitors. And you'll want them to have tablets or laptops or even towers depending on their need for mobility. There's bad news and good news for small business owners modernizing their technology.

Here's the bad news:

- You must guard against digital theft.
- You must look as professional and perform as well as the big guys.
- You must learn fast and keep up with rapid tech changes.

But the good news is very good:

- Most software is cloud-based, with versions designed for small businesses at affordable prices.
- More functions are integrated and purchased together.
- It's not so hard to look as professional and perform as well (or better!) than the big guys.

Protect Your Data

Since you opened your doors, "cybersecurity" has become a household word. As a business owner, you have a responsibility to safeguard information that you collect about your employees and your customers, plus you must protect all your important records and business assets.

Whatever you do with technology, take precautions about how and where you collect, store, and retrieve data and train your employees to do the same. For example:

- Use a secure password on every device
- Never share passwords, and require password changes quarterly
- Handle credit cards and receipts properly
- Turn devices off when you leave
- Carefully control how data folders are shared or restricted
- Have a good back-up process for all your data

If your assistant is going to manage e-mail and social media accounts for you, choose software that allows for that practice rather than having someone else log in as if he were you. Always get the right tools for the job the way you intend to do it.

Big Choices

I recommend that you set up your office (or back office) to be mobile enabled. That way, as you grow, it's easy to move or add employees in different locations, employ freelancers or integrate outsource partners anywhere in the world, and work wherever you are or want to be. Here are some ideas:

- **Virtual Phone System**
  A virtual phone system provides you with local and toll-free phone numbers, an answering service, call forwarding to you or any of your employees' cell phones, voice mail, voice

mail to text, and other services. Choose a service based on your business size, options offered, and price.

- **Google Voice**
- **Grasshopper** (grasshopper.com)
- **Nextiva.com**

- **Virtual Office Address**
  You can have an office address to send and receive mail anywhere in the country, plus there are services where you can rent an office or conference room as you need one in any major city. You pay only when you use the service. No one knows if you typically work from your dining room table or your garage!

Personal FIX
Melinda's Top Four Personal Productivity Apps

Nozbe: Is a task-management system for your cell phone that lets small business owners keep track of what you've delegated and what you've assigned to yourself. You can e-mail it tasks to add. The app also integrates with Evernote and Dropbox.

Ifttt: Is short for "If this, then that," Ifttt is a simple web app that automates actions when certain conditions are met. Ifttt can also automatically bookmark blog posts from your favorite blogs for you to read later and call with appointment reminders.

Coffee break app: If you are one of those entrepreneurs (like me) that gets into "the zone" and barely remembers to eat lunch or take a break, this app reminds you. Studies show your brain becomes less effective if you don't take a break every 90 minutes, and this app is here to save you from yourself. Every 90 minutes it locks your computer until you close your eyes or get some fresh air. Unfortunately, it only works on a Mac, but it's a lifesaver for workaholics.

Freedom: An app that allows you to block websites and apps from any of your devices whenever you want to stay focused to get something done. Set your own focus times or let the app keep you honest.

Office Management Suite and Collaboration Tools

Basic document tools for word processing, spreadsheets, and slide presentations come in all flavors from competing operating systems—Microsoft Word, Excel, and PowerPoint; Apple Pages and Keynote; Google Docs, Sheets, and Slides. Today, they are virtually interchangeable between machines and systems, and many other vendors make compatible versions. By the time you read this, the standards may have blended even more or new universal standards may have taken their place. What's best for your business, however, is an integrated internal system that facilitates powerful data sharing and collaboration among your team. Here are three cloud-based integrated office systems that represent what's available.

- **G-Suite**
  Google's G-Suite service includes Google Docs, Gmail, Calendar, and Contacts. You can store, share, and sync on Google Drive. It has video and voice conferencing. You can also add sites and apps. It has tons of storage and a great reputation for security. You can also export and share files with people who don't use G-Suite. It is very inexpensive; designed for small business and start-ups.

- **Microsoft Office 365 Business Premium**
  This suite will grow with your company as big as you want to get. You subscribe per user, per month, and you

get a lot for your money. The learning curve is higher than others. Don't go this route unless you have several employees and intend to grow. It offers all the basic production tools, robust e-mail, calendar, and contact management. Excellent note-taking, document storage, research tools, and superior team collaboration tools with SharePoint, Skype for Business, and Exchange Server, which is especially designed for multiple teams with many projects. It offers add-ons for CRM, web hosting, and more.

- **Zoho One (zoho.com)**
  Zoho One includes more than 35 applications with complementary mobile apps so you can run your entire business on one suite. They offer full-featured, enterprise editions of the entire Zoho suite. That means being able to reach customers, grow sales, balance your books, and work in productive and collaborative ways, manage HR and business processes from any device—all with a single login and password. Prices start very low and grow by the number of employees and range of services you use.

Accounting Software

If your accounting software isn't part of your office suite, choose one that is compatible—preferably one that can be integrated and works with your bank and credit card company easily. QuickBooks online is an industry standard, but there are many others to choose from including Sage One and FreshBooks, etc.

Payment Processing

Square.com and **PayPal Here** are the major titans of on-the-go mobile-payment devices that plug right into your smartphone or tablet headphone jack to accept credit card payments. Square and PayPal both supply mobile card readers and apps. The basic free reader from both companies charge a fee for a chip card reader.

Square charges a fixed percent per transaction of 2.75%, but they process payment overnight. PayPal charges a fixed percent per transaction of 2.70%, and PayPal Here will also process checks. Both can have 2-3 days to receive your payment. Square's customer service is virtually non-existent; they only offer online support. PayPal provides phone, e-mail, and online support for its users.

Customer Relationship Software (CRM)

Ideally, your customer database will be part of your office suite or integrate with it. As you grow, your CRM needs will become more complex because you'll want to track more information about your customers and your firm's interactions. You'll want to be able to reach them through all your social media channels as well as their mailing addresses. There's a big difference in CRM needs for a B2B and a B2C company. Different types of companies require different types of CRMs. Think about future growth when you make CRM decisions. Choose something that's easy to export data so you can move easily if you need to change vendors.

Mini FIX
CRM OPTIONS

A good CRM will fulfill multiple functions for your business. When you are deciding which one is best for you, consider first what functions will be most useful to your business. This will simplify your decision:

- Marketing—you have robust e-mail marketing and selling online, you are building web traffic, sales funnels, and upsells, you are deep into social media and content marketing
- Sales—you have a sales team, you need to manage leads and customer contacts, monitor your sales process, make sales forecasts

---

> - Customer service—you have a customer service team who handles customer trouble tickets, schedules and follows up on service calls
> - Contact management—you want all customer data in one place to streamline data entry

At the moment, Salesforce.com, Zoho CRM, and Hubspot.com seem to dominate the CRM market, with Zoho CRM especially dedicated to small businesses. But you have dozens, if not hundreds of choices. Now if you have never used a CRM system, I would suggest getting started with Insightly.com. It's inexpensive and works well for a 1-4-person business. You'll find big pricing differences in CRMs as well as differences in performance specialties. Be sure you are looking at your big picture before you make a price-based decision. A lower initial price that requires lots of add-ons won't pay off long-term.

That covers the basic tools that every business needs as it grows. I want to add a few more very popular apps that are huge time savers.

- **Evernote—STAY ORGANIZED**
  This easy-to-use, free app helps you stay organized across all your devices. It lets you take notes, sync files, save web pages, capture photos, create to-do lists, and record voice reminders. It generates receipts on the go. And it makes all these tasks completely searchable, whether you're at home, at work, or on the go. The small business owners I surveyed said it's the best productivity app out there!

- **Dropbox—STORE AND SHARE FILES**
  This free (or paid professional) cloud-based, file-storing service lets you bring your photos, docs, and videos anywhere and share them easily with your laptop or mobile device. No more danger from the blue screen of death with this app. Move all your files to the cloud so you can access them

from any device, anywhere. You can also interface with your team to share files, which provides great version control and cuts down on e-mail.

- **PASSWORD MANAGER AND FORM FILLER**
  Try **LastPass** or **Dashlane**. This kind of tool enables you to use very secure passwords and change them frequently, but relieves the stress of trying to remember a slew of passwords. If you regularly move between multiple computers, devices, and operating systems, use a system that securely stores and gives you access to any of your account credentials.

- **TEAM COLLABORATION**
  Sometimes texting, e-mail, or even Google Hangouts doesn't cut it for inter-office communication. **Zoom** or **Slack** are communication software that lets you organize chats into channels, upload and share files, or search your message archive. It also has great phone apps that let you stay in touch with your team on the go.

EXPERT INTERVIEW

Leveraging the Right Tools for Your Small Business
Candid interview with productivity expert Laura Stack

Where should you start developing a technology hit list in your business?

You should look at the practices and processes that are manual, time-consuming, or inefficient. Spend the day paying attention to everything you do, and where you hit snags. If you're hesitant to spend money on software solutions, consider how many hours a day you're wasting doing things inefficiently. Isn't it worth it to spend $20 a month (as an example) to save seven hours a month?

There are so many apps and tech tools out there, it's hard to know what is best. Do you have best practices on picking productivity tools?

First ask other entrepreneurs for recommendations. Then, look for reviews online. Just about any software you can consider has been reviewed on multiple websites. Then finally, test the software before you buy. Most solutions offer free trials, which gives you a few weeks to assess whether it solves the problem you have.

What are your top technology time-savers?

A. **Social Media & Analytics:** Social media management dashboards can allow you to schedule social updates in advance so you're not logging into multiple accounts all day long. I use **SproutSocial** and **Hootsuite** to manage all my social media accounts in one place, as well as to schedule my updates in advance. I also like it because it gives me insights into which shares and updates were the most popular. Also use **Google Analytics** to give you a sense of who's visiting your site, what pages they're looking at, and where they're exiting before buying.

B. **Computer Use & Document Management:** To save time when using my computer, I use **Shortkeys.com**. When I share documents with my team, several of us may need to make changes to a document. We use **Google Docs** and project management software such as **Teamwork** or **Slack** because it manages version control and everyone can make changes to the same shared document.

C. **Customer Relationship Management:** When you have clients, it's important that you stay on top of the conversations you've had with them, as well as have their contact information at the ready. CRM software will also help monitor the productivity of your sales reps. Try **ACT CRM, marketing360** or **Insightly** for CRM solutions.

D. **E-mail:** When it comes to e-mail, **MailChimp.com** and **Weber.com** are good when you are just getting started with e-mail marketing, but once you build a significant list, and are ready to generate revenue through e-mail, try **Infusionsoft.com.**

E-mail is a big nightmare for many business owners. How do you suggest we get e-mail under control?
Use my 6D System©: Discard, Delegate, Do, Date, Drawer, or Deter. I suggest setting hours for yourself for when you will check e-mail. When you're done with the work day, be done checking e-mail. Maybe turn off e-mail notifications on your phone. When you check e-mail, spend say, an hour, then go on to other activities. This will help you focus 100% on the task you're doing, rather than switching back and forth between tasks.

You are a fan of outsourcing. What are your top resources to find freelancers and virtual support staff?
I like to post on social media when I have a job opening, but many entrepreneurs who hire freelancers use both **UpWork** and **Craigslist.**

What kinds of agreements do you need to have in place to protect your business from virtual team members?
If you have any information that you are worried a freelancer might steal, have them sign a non-disclosure document. This will protect your proprietary information. It's also good to use a contract that outlines the scope of work, delivery timeline, and payment terms, and that you are hiring them as work-for-hire which means you own their work product. If you need to give virtual team members access to project management software or accounts (like social media, for example), be sure to change those passwords once those people stop working for you.

What is your best advice for business owners who want to figure out how to do less and make more money?
Become more efficient with systems. Create a foundational time management, scheduling, task list, and e-mail handling system that everything else builds upon.

About the Expert

Laura Stack is the President & CEO of The Productivity Pro, Inc., a boutique consulting firm helping leaders increase workplace performance in high-stress environments. Her latest book is, *Doing the Right Things Right: How the Effective Executive Spends Time*. For more information, go to www.theproductivitypro.com.

FIX YOUR PRODUCTIVITY

Make a list of productivity tools that you personally need to start using. Start with your Process lists in Chapter 5: Which processes can you automate with technology?

Conduct an audit of the technology tools your business is using right now and how much you are paying monthly or annually. (Ask your bookkeeper to do this task for you.) At a staff meeting, ask each employee about other tools they use independently. Determine the total cost of your business technology and see what you can streamline, ditch, or upgrade.

Ask your team what they are missing in the way of technology tools. What could help them work more efficiently? Review your Process worksheets (Chapter Five) for background.

FIX YOUR BUSINESS ACTION STEPS

Take these steps and add your own based on Chapter 6: Productivity.

1. What productivity software and/or hardware do you need for your company?

2. Prioritize your list of needs.

   a)

   b)

   c)

   d)

   e)

3. Make a plan to review software options, or select an employee to explore options and make recommendations to you. Engage a consultant if you need one.

4. Due to cost and business disruption, do you need to phase in the technology upgrade?

5. Build a Strategic Plan for your long-term technology needs.

CHAPTER 7: PERFORMANCE
MEASURE YOUR RESULTS

People typically do business with you because of one of these three things:

- Cheaper
- Better
- Faster

If your value proposition is stronger than that offered by competitors, you win. Value is a comparison of the benefits you offer relative to price. To attract ready, willing, and able buyers, you must develop a brand and solutions that appeal to specific buyers, then communicate your message through marketing channels. Another perspective is that people buy things to address a need or solve a problem. You succeed if you can do it best! Here are several of the most compelling reasons that people might choose to do business with you.

Brand Reputation or Earned Trust

It doesn't happen overnight, but if you can build a business and brand that people trust, half the battle is complete. When comparing options in a buying scenario, people tend to lean on a trusted name when all else seems equal.

From day one, focus your small business marketing on establishing credibility and the reputation you seek. If you want to be known as an elite customer service provider, for instance, ensure that you deliver a quality experience that easily stands out from what people normally get elsewhere. The more consistently you solve problems for targeted buyers, the stronger your image of credibility and expertise gets.

An Elite Solution

An elite solution is one in which the product and service deliver a combination of benefits far superior to most alternatives. A certain portion of the market in most industries only wants one thing – the best possible solution.

Whether you make your own products or source them from suppliers, you can almost guarantee a foundation of buyers if you deliver a stellar solution. One main reason for this reality is that superior benefits are among the easiest small business marketing messages to convey. An even better way to compel particular buyers is to offer an exclusive product or service. People are always attracted to things other people can't easily get.

Convenience or Efficiency

In some cases, customers sacrifice top quality in exchange for convenience or efficiency. For instance, people who go through the McDonald's drive-through, often do so based on the convenience of the location and efficiency of the service, not the quality of the food.

A convenient location and a timely purchase process are key factors to satisfying busy or rushed customers. A compelling reason to present your business through e-commerce is because of the convenience it offers. You can attract people who prefer to order from home or on the road without having to visit a store. Kiosk locations are another way current businesses expand their reach and offer a convenient solution.

A Safe and Comfortable Experience

People are emotional creatures. You have the ability to attract buyers by appealing to many emotions. Showing empathy for the problems your buyers face and addressing them with your product or service offerings is a great place to start. Beyond that, many people prefer a safe and comfortable buying experience versus one that is uncertain, complex, frustrating, or risky.

In a traditional brick-and-mortar operation, you can control the experience through merchandising, layout, lighting, and check out stations. Online, easy navigation, clear organization, and a frictionless shopping cart process contribute to a comfortable and quick shopping experience. Protecting the privacy and security of your buyers is also important.

Other Factors That Attract Buyers

In addition to these major reasons people buy from you, consider the following as other opportunities to attract buyers:

- Clear communication of value
- Mission driven
- Local community involvement
- Sustainability or "green" practices

The ultimate reason people come to your business is because you best address their problem or need. In developing and marketing your small business, consider which special strengths you have and how they speak to the target market. When you can best provide specific benefits to an underserved market, you have a compelling value proposition.

Under-promise and Over-deliver

How well you connect with your customers through your products, services, and support will determine whether they come back and buy from you repeatedly. But even if you sell the most amazing products ever, there's still room to improve your customer service. One strategy is to under-promise and over-deliver. What do I mean by that?

Some may tell you to think of under-promising what you can give a customer as an "in case of emergency" cushion for worst-case scenarios, but it's better to plan for success than for failure. By promising one thing (five-day delivery, for example) and beating expectations with two-day delivery) you'll surprise and delight your customers. And that will keep them coming back. Here are four ways to ensure that your customers are constantly enchanted with your service, plus one freebie tip for the customer who cannot be satisfied.

When you thank your customers for business, ask for feedback.

One way to know how to over-deliver to your customers and also gain valuable insight is to ask your customers what they want. Institute an outreach program that connects with customers within 7-10 days after the transaction is complete. Ask your customer to provide specific ratings and input on a few specific topics. Then look at trends. If you constantly hear that your product isn't well-packaged and gets damaged in shipping, that's something you can take direct action to improve.

Leverage Your CRM

If you've ever called a customer service line, been transferred, and then had to re-explain your situation, you no doubt were frustrated that the company didn't keep better records on your past interactions with it. Delight your customers by storing detailed records on past transactions and calls with CRM.

Anyone with access to the software can become an expert in your customer's history quickly and painlessly—and instantly improve your customer's experience.

Surprise Them with a Gesture

There are many ways to acknowledge your appreciation for your customer's business. You might add a few pieces of candy in the shipment box, send a handwritten thank you note or offer a small discount code if she purchases again within a short time frame. It is important to let your customer know that her business is important to you and that you value it. The incentive or gift is just the icing on top.

How to Handle Unhappy Customers

Unhappy customers are part of running a small business. No matter how pleasant your personality or good your service delivery, someone will eventually criticize your product, staff, packaging, or even your response to their complaint. So how do you respond to unhappy customers in your small business?

Part of you might want to tell the customer to kick rocks. After all, you have other customers, right? However, that strategy will only lead to a damaged reputation, lost revenue, and a nasty online review about your business. Even though an unhappy customer creates an unpleasant situation, I recommend these strategies to resolve customer complaints.

Force Yourself to Listen

Nobody wakes up in the morning and thinks, "Today I hope I get screamed at by an irate customer." However, it might happen, and you must be ready for it. The key is to be patient and listen to them. Unhappy customers need to vent. They feel they've been wronged, and if you interrupt them, you'll only anger them further. Instead of shutting down the tirade, practice active listening. Take in everything they say and try to separate the words from the emotion, so you can figure out how to solve the problem.

Ask Questions

While you shouldn't talk over an angry customer, you should wait for a break in his or her explanation to ask questions. Clarify any details that you don't understand so you can get the full picture. It's also helpful to grab a pad and pen to take notes. Let the customer know that you want to get his or her complaint exactly right. Asking questions can also help you find a resolution. You might say, "I understand that you're unhappy with the quality of the product. Is there anything we can do to win back your trust?"

This puts the ball in your customer's court. It's okay if he or she doesn't have a response, but the customer might take the weight off your shoulders by describing exactly what will rectify the problem.

Handling Abusive Customers

Unhappy customers often exaggerate the situation and use abusive language to get their point across. Even if the customer uses colorful language, don't go there. Try to get clear on the source of their rage. After you've heard out your customer, try to forget about the abusive language by putting yourself in their shoes. You'll only make yourself angry by dwelling on it. Instead, focus on the root of the problem so that you can find a solution. So that you can learn something to help your business run better. Often things like this can lead to better staff training. After all, honest feedback is a gift.

Resolve the Problem

You must be the boss. If the customer makes an unreasonable request, just say yes. Even if it's hard, just say yes. People will forget what you say, but they will tell everyone how you made them feel. You can't please everyone, but I believe you should never let a customer down.

Quick FIX
Handling negative online reviews

You need to know how to deal with negative online reviews, because too often small business owners ignore those reviews, when with a little work, you can turn them around. Follow these steps:

- **Use Google Alerts.** You need to know when something is posted about your business.
- **Don't get mad.** Most people will react negatively to a negative review, but that's the worst thing you can do. Instead, apologize to the customer for what went wrong, explain that you want to correct the situation, and then ask the customer to contact you—offline.
- **Don't argue, listen.** Most customers want empathy more than a refund.
- **Resolve the problem.** Follow through to get the problem fixed.
- **Correct the record.** If you think you've diffused the situation, ask the customer if they would remove the negative review.

You can resolve any customer service issue with the right language and attitude. It is awesome when you can turn an angry customer into a loyal ambassador for your brand. Follow some of the strategies I've used successfully in my business:

Go beyond the customer's expectations. Don't just solve the problem. Give them more than they asked for: refund their money and offer FREE coupons for a return visit. Call them in a week and again in a month to make sure everything is good with their purchase. They will become your best brand ambassadors.

Never lose your smile. Staying pleasant is powerful. Pretend you're talking to a thrilled client instead of a disappointed one.

Work quickly. Don't make customers wait for a resolution. Empower your employees to resolve issues up to $500.00, without approval.

If you make customer happiness your top priority, your customers will come back again and again. Sometimes the customer really isn't right. But, if you want to stay in business, I think it's essential to know how to work with all types of people—even the unreasonable ones.

Customer Surveys

Customer satisfaction is an important element of small business growth. But do you measure customer satisfaction regularly? Conducting a customer survey is not an end in itself, but it is the beginning of a process that should show you actionable ways to improve your business.

Surveys that measure customer satisfaction should be a regular part of your business practice. With specific enough questions, your customers can indicate to you how your business is functioning. A survey will also indicate which areas must be adjusted or changed to improve your business and generate more repeat business. You can ask questions about price, value, your staff, and the availability of products to measure your business operations.

Quick FIX
QUICK WAYS TO DO CUSTOMER SURVEYS

- SurveyMonkey.com—It has great templates with proven questions, integrates with your e-mail client, has easy ways to analyze data, has nice reporting tools
- Facebook survey—It's easy, you can get more Likes on your page as well, do it often
- Facebook poll—You can ask a new question each week!
- Google Forms—It's super easy, great with Google contacts, has easy data dump to spreadsheet

---

How Surveys Can Fuel Growth

While your customer surveys should ask questions about the goods and services you offer and the way your business functions, surveys can also be used to help grow the business. Start by including questions about potential new products and services to gauge interest. Allow customer input to help you decide which new goods and services to add. Getting early buy-in from customers can also generate excitement and anticipation for new products before they even launch.

Another way surveys can fuel growth is by giving an accurate picture of what customers really think of your business. Identifying strengths and weaknesses in your sales and customer experience will help you improve, which will lead to happier customers and more sales.

Just sending a survey to customers via e-mail, text, or phone can help boost sales by keeping the business's name in the forefront of clients' minds, so they will be more likely to purchase in the future, especially if you give them an incentive for completing the survey. After all, people love free stuff.

Surveys Give a Competitive Advantage

When your customers are happy, they are less likely to look elsewhere for their products and services. Your competitive advantage comes from the ability to tell where customers are coming from and to know their likes and dislikes, needs and wants. Satisfied customers are loyal customers, and your competitors are not likely to woo them away from you when you know them so well.

Customer Service Training

When you have an effective survey process, you can train employees to meet customer needs more efficiently. You want to specifically advise and empower them on the best ways to build relationships with customers as they serve them. Increased customer loyalty is one by-product of the survey process.

Surveys do not just reveal weaknesses; they also reveal strengths. Customer satisfaction is not just about improving weak areas, but also about playing up areas of strength so the business can become even stronger. Knowing what you are doing right and wrong is the first step to changing and improving the business.

Some of your employees may engage with customers face-to-face, in a restaurant or clinic or retail store. Others engage via phone or Skype or e-mail, chat, social media, or text, but still directly; one-on-one or in small groups, they need coaching on selling and problem-solving. How you train them to interact with your customers is the key to your brand reputation. In fact, your entire value proposition is delivered to your customers through your employees.

First, it's important that every employee understand how you expect them to treat a customer and how you want them to handle problems. But even beyond that, your company culture determines how employees treat customers.

Other Customer Experience Data

Many small business owners rely on our guts or intuition to make major business decisions. Many of us feel we can't afford Big Data solutions to provide complicated analytics and metrics for decision making. It's not as complicated or expensive as it might seem, and the data has a valuable place in the decision-making process.

Don't let the term "*data*" scare you. It's just another word for information, and we can all benefit from information, right? With the right data, you can use past sales, web traffic, or marketing campaign click-throughs to drive future decisions about those areas.

Let's say you are trying to decide where to put more money for your next marketing effort. In the past, you tried LinkedIn ads, but they didn't generate many sales. You did better with the free download you offered to customers on your Facebook page. You can look at your data from each of these efforts to decide if you want to create a new download offer, since you had success in the past. Or maybe you want to try another channel like e-mail or ads on Instagram, if you haven't tried before.

We've all made decisions based on our gut before, but when it comes to something as important as your marketing efforts, that is measurable, and you make the most informed decisions based on the data that's available to you.

Decide What Data Matter

There is a ton of data available to us right now, but let me let you in on a secret: you can ignore 99% of it. Just because you can measure everything from the sentiment of your social media followers to what country people visiting your site came from doesn't mean this information is essential to your decision making. Here are a few of the data metrics that might be important to you:

Web Traffic

- Which sources send the most web traffic to your site?
- Which content converts the best for the site?
- What are the most popular pages on the site?
- How fast do people leave your site?

Sales

- Which sales funnels are driving the most sales?
- Which products are selling the best/worst?
- To what price point do people respond best?

Marketing

- Which marketing channels net the most leads?
- What is the closest ratio of online leads?
- Which paid marketing efforts have the best ROI?

If you're trying to decide what to do to increase sales, for example, look at the data that are most relevant to your decision.

In addition to customer survey information, past sales data, product information, and your marketing channels will all play a part in what you decide.

Use Data Wisely

Data is only useful if you put it to work. Knowing that, for example, if 45% of your web traffic comes from your guest blogging efforts, it's useless if you don't use that information to bring even more people to your site. Knowing that a large percentage of your customers are abandoning their shopping carts before completing a purchase won't change unless you get to the bottom of why they're leaving.

Mini FIX
REASONS CUSTOMERS ABANDON THEIR SHOPPING CARTS

How many of these factors are issues on your e-commerce website?

- They're just looking
- They're forced to register
- They're comparing prices
- It's too complicated
- Not enough payment options
- Shipping is too expensive
- Shipping cost isn't revealed until the end
- Not enough shipping options
- Product plus tax and shipping is too high
- Item isn't available right away
- Technical issues
- Not enough product information on the site
- They're going to buy it in the store
- Product is too expensive
- Fears about their data security
- Can't find coupons

Employee Engagement

Today's small businesses are increasingly focused on culture as one of their competitive differentiators. That's because research points to the many ways developing a great culture can engage and attract great employees, eventually resulting in a healthier bottom line. Recognition and appreciation are two simple ways of building employee loyalty, but alone they're not sufficient.

If you want employees who aren't just engaged in their work, but fiercely loyal, it's a good idea to start out by understanding how strong engagement is associated with business innovation.

Continuous improvement, ongoing innovation, and customer satisfaction all rest on excellent employee engagement and loyalty. In fact, many companies have concluded that checking employee engagement and motivation frequently can have a preventative effect on unpredictable events that tend to knock employee morale off its feet.

An engaged team is one that isn't afraid to innovate, even if it involves a certain amount of risk-taking. Not all those risks will pay off, of course, but employees who don't feel hamstrung by blame game politics, restrictive policies, or by a "That's the way we've always done it" mentality are more likely to move the business forward with innovative products, services, and customer relationships.

Faster time-to-market can be a strong differentiator for a small business. The agility with which a smaller business operates is an advantage in today's dynamic marketplace compared with huge organizations that simply can't turn on a dime. Leading HR experts have discovered that when employee motivation is tracked alongside traditional metrics like development speed of new products, employee engagement problems generally don't have time to manifest. Some believe that poor employee engagement is a leading indicator rather than a lagging indicator of problems like missed deadlines, unexpected resignations, or product problems.

Pre FIX
PREPARING FOR CRISIS MANAGEMENT

You never know when you could be faced with a customer relations crisis. From product tampering to employee missteps to vendor problems and policy disasters, you've seen big companies get hit with this everywhere. Wells Fargo, Toyota, United Airlines, and so many more. How can you protect your company?

- Have a crisis management plan, put together with professional help. (Take an online course or hire a consultant.)
- Get media training for yourself. Learn how to handle yourself in front of a camera in a challenging or hostile interview.
- Identify a PR person or firm skilled in crisis communications whom you would hire in a crisis.
- Train your team to avoid a crisis, to recognize a crisis in the making, and the protocol to follow in a crisis.

Investment in Employee Appreciation Is Wise

Employee appreciation is an investment that pays off, literally and figuratively. A recent SHRM/Globoforce survey found that the most effective employee appreciation and recognition programs were ones that spent more than 1% of payroll on employee recognition rewards. Previous studies have reported that companies that do this show better results overall. Researchers theorize that it is because employees need to have tangible proof of their value to the organization along with communication of messages of appreciation. Spending more than 1% of payroll on such recognition can improve workforce cohesiveness and loyalty.

"Employee engagement" may feel like just another business buzzword, but it is actually much more than that. Whether you call it employee engagement, morale, or motivation, businesses of every size have learned that poor employee engagement, where work is 100% business and 0% personal, has become an epidemic that has negatively affected business performance.

Teamwork and cohesion require mutual trust and great communication, including public recognition when someone accomplishes something noteworthy. Ideally, you want your small business to go from employee engagement to something more like an employee lovefest where you can envision your team working happily ever after. It all starts with keeping in touch with the needs of your team personally and for the business.

EXPERT INTERVIEW

Measuring Results in Your Small Business
Candid interview with restaurateur and author Misty Young

What are the top ways small businesses should measure results?

I'm a strong believer in measurement. Anything measured improves. More importantly, *anything measured and reported, improves even faster*. Everyone wants to succeed and more information helps meet that important goal. Small businesses are often so wrapped up in the "doing" of their businesses they're not paying attention to the *development* of their businesses—to their peril. So, what should be measured?

Start by identifying the low hanging fruit: How many dollars are coming in? Daily? Weekly? Monthly? Annually? How many dollars are going out for expenses during those same periods? Measure how many clients/patrons/customers/patients pay you, come in physically, or make a purchase online during those periods? Measure the timing of the highest business volume. Does your staffing match the business volume? Are there times when people spend more money? Are weekend sales the same as weekday sales? Are holiday numbers the same as regular days? What are the differences in purchases?

Once you've measured these basics, move to the higher fruit, measure your cost of client acquisition, or the cost to get a new client. What method of client acquisition is the most productive and which is least? What can you do more of? Keep in mind that minutes are money, measure your staff and your own time down to the minute and spend money this way. Spend as little as possible, but as much as necessary to make the sale. Efficiency matters! As you get better at measuring one thing, you'll get better at measuring all things.

How can you build a great customer service program and train your team to implement it?
Training is the ultimate fulfillment of your brand promise, no matter the business you are in. Find your industry's best books and buy them for your team. Pay them to read or listen to the book as part of their weekly duties and have a mastermind session weekly to brainstorm ideas and hear feedback. Ask your team to serve each other first and foremost. When they have an internal service focus, they'll automatically want to help the clients even more. When your entire team knows the goal, the direction, and isn't trying to read your mind, your customer service will vastly improve. Be sure to celebrate wins to help team building—use every client downfall as a training opportunity to build your team.

Do the same rules apply for e-commerce businesses, retailers, and professional service businesses with customer service?
Yes! These are the rules no matter what business you're in:

- Kindness
- Courtesy
- Honesty
- Efficient product or service fulfillment
- Gratitude

That's it.

If a business wants to enhance their customer experience pre-sale, how is it done?
The best way to make a sale today is to make the pre-sale before you meet the buyer—give them as much relevant information as you can. Educate them in every aspect of your product or service, respect their time and ask for the sale. Every modern business must have a comprehensive, integrated digital presence with a website, social channels, testimonials, links to reviews, fabulous photography, descriptive language and potentially an app. All pre-marketing material must be solid with factual information,

detailed infographics, appealing optics, interesting, relevant videos to meet your buyers where they are in the information gathering stage. You've got to make more information available than ever before.

And when the buyer is in front of you, get right to the point. Thank them for taking the time to come in (or click-through) and ask how you can serve them, what specifically do they need, and what do they want? Rapport building is old-school.

Are surveys the right strategy to get feedback and how often should they be done?
Surveys are an excellent tool for feedback. Do them as often as you can. In one of our businesses, we do them, literally DAILY. Surveys can help you identify areas of strength, recognize and reward your staff for excellence, and shine a light on opportunities for improvement and training.

What's your best advice for business owners who want to reinvent their business model?
You get what you settle for. You can make your business better. Information-based decisions will help you look at your business with "new eyes." Ultimately, the truth of your business is not what you sell. You are not in the breakfast business or the floral business, and you're not in the marketing business. *We are all in the people business.*

About the Expert

Misty Young was a press secretary to a governor and attorney general and VP/Partner in a marketing firm before buying a struggling restaurant near Lake Tahoe, California. Since then she's built a regional chain of Squeeze In breakfast/lunch restaurants and is now Board Chair of Squeeze In Franchising, LLC. She's also the author of *From Rags to Restaurants* and the co-founder of YoungSocial, a digital marketing agency. For more information, go to www.squeezein.com.

FIX YOUR PERFORMANCE

EMERSON'S URGENCIES:
SEEK HELP IMMEDIATELY!

What Top 5 things will you start to measure in your small business?

1.
2.
3.
4.
5.

What can you do in the next 90 days to boost employee engagement?

1.
2.
3.

How would you rate the customer service of your team? Make a list of things you'd like to address in upcoming training sessions.

1.
2.
3.
4.
5.

Make a note of other items from this chapter that you want to add to your Strategic Plan.

FIX YOUR PERFORMANCE ACTION STEPS

Take these steps and add your own based on Chapter 7: Performance.

Discuss the customer experience with your team. What is their sense of how good it is? What do they think needs improvement? What would they like to learn from a survey?
Make plans for one or a series of customer surveys. Decide how to conduct them and who will be in charge. Get the ball rolling.
Brainstorm with your team 3-5 ways you can Under-promise and Over-deliver for your customers.
Ask your team how they want their hard work acknowledged. Some may want money, time off, recognition, or more visible projects. This is important to know especially when you can't afford cash bonuses.
Decide how to include customer experience knowledge into your Strategic Planning process.

CHAPTER 8: PRODUCT
IS YOUR BUSINESS STILL RELEVANT?

In the early years of your business, you struggled to find a foothold in a competitive industry. Then, you found your target customers and enjoy success. But what few entrepreneurs ever bother asking themselves a few years down the road is: Is my business still relevant? Do I still have a customer base that will support me for years to come? Am I in an industry that is growing or shrinking? Are there any new competitors or technology that are changing my industry?

Apple is a great example of such a competitor. Before the iPhone, we had cell phones with no features other than the ability to talk and text. There were also MP3 players so we could listen to our tunes on the go. But the iPhone killed both these markets and created a new device that did what the other two markets did—only better. And they added the camera and opened the door for other innovators to create apps for them! You should be constantly on guard for innovation that will change your industry and potentially put you out of business. And, you should be constantly on the lookout for an innovation that can propel you in the marketplace!

Be Honest with Yourself About Your Brand

You may have performed a SWOT analysis when you first started your company—that's your brand's Strengths, Weaknesses, Opportunities, and Threats—but the landscape has likely changed since then. Make it a part of your annual strategy exercise with your team to look at your brand objectively.

- Where do we now stand among other competitors?
- What benefits do we offer over the others?
- Where are we weak?
- What innovations have put our products or services at risk?

This activity can really open your eyes, if you're not as well-positioned in your industry as you think you are. The purpose here is to get a measurement of where you are. The next step is to do something to improve your standing in the marketplace.

Be Open to Change

Being stuck in your ways won't win you more market share. As digital cameras rose in popularity a few decades ago, the film company Kodak was very slow to adapt, eventually filing for bankruptcy in 2012. If technology is disrupting your industry, will your existing products or services become extinct? Or are there ways you can incorporate modern tools to make them even more competitive? Don't stick your head in the sand and assume everything will be all right. Any business unwilling to adapt to change will soon be forgotten.

Quick FIX
COMPARE YOUR COMPETETIVE ADVANTAGE

Ask your marketing person to visit the websites of your key competitors, locally and in places that you'd like to expand.

Copy key phrases and statements that capture their value proposition, brand promise, or other competitive advantages they offer.

Put your competitors' statements side by side with statements from your own website and other marketing and sales materials.

Review yours vs. theirs. Do you promise anything unique? Anything different? Do you offer greater value for the money? A better guarantee? More service?

Ask your kitchen cabinet and your team.

Ask Your Customers

If you're simply not sure how relevant your company is, talk to your customers. Ask questions on social media. Try focus groups. Talk to your staff, particularly your salespeople. Conversations can open the door to insight into what your customers want and let you know whether you're still delivering it or not. Your website analytics are also a help here. Pay special attention to which pages people are visiting the most and which they're visiting the least. The latter may indicate that those products are no longer as relevant and may be worth discontinuing.

We all face the potential of becoming irrelevant if we don't continue to innovate and grow. Stay tapped into your industry trends. Let nothing come as a surprise. Be willing to take risks and try new things to remain a necessity for your customers.

Your Competitive Advantage

No matter what industry you're in, I'm willing to bet it's competitive. You constantly have to be on your toes and know what the other players in your field are doing. However, it helps if you have a strong competitive advantage. This is that *je ne sais quoi* that makes your brand unique and attracts customers to you. If you don't know what your competitive advantage is, I will help you find it as well as help you keep it.

Defining What Makes You Unique

Not sure what your competitive advantage is? Here are several examples:

- You offer products no one else does
- You focus on high-end quality products
- You offer stellar customer service
- You charge less
- You offer a quick turnaround
- You offer a unique in-home experience

If you were to ask your customers why they come back to you repeatedly, what would they say? Don't be shy to ask them this exact question. Sometimes you're too close to your business to see what your advantage is, and your customers' answers may surprise you.

Shift Your Mindset About Your Competitors

A wise woman once told me, "Never underestimate your opponent." Even if you've got an amazing competitive advantage, it's important to not rest on your laurels and assume you will always be on top. It's easy to mimic those benefits your company offers, and if you're thriving, you should expect that other companies will do just that.

When business is booming, it's easy to think you'll never hit a downturn. However, nothing lasts forever. A lower price or deeper relationship could always cause you to lose your biggest contract. When your competitors are light years behind you or you put all your energy into one large client, you take your focus away from that competitive advantage, even though you shouldn't. Have the attitude that your competitive advantage is something you must fight for, every day.

Sustaining Your Edge

Once you accept that your competitive advantage is something you can never take for granted, you've got to be diligent about keeping your customers. If your advantage is offering the best product on the market, make sure you're paying attention to all other players and the quality of their products. Continue to innovate on your own products and services, too. If customer service is your strong suit, make sure your staff has continual training, and that you monitor a few calls to ensure they're following your high-quality customer service protocol. Remember, sustaining that competitive advantage takes effort. If it's truly important to you to own that advantage, put energy into maintaining it every day.

Refining Your Niche

If you've built your business focusing on a concentration of clients in an area of limited competition, you've spent your time generating business and less time looking for the market. But sometimes the market can move away from you. Remember when you had to hire a lawyer to do things such as incorporating your business, developing a will, or drafting a partnership agreement? Now, you can do all that online for a fraction of the cost of hiring a lawyer. I bet many lawyers didn't see that coming. It is natural for a target market to change over the course of a business; you just have to be willing to adjust with it. It's important to build solid client relationships that operate in a partnership mode. If you find yourself needing to refine your target market, here are a few things to consider.

Focus on the business relationships you enjoy: With which clients do you really enjoy working? These are the ones where you make a difference and they value your hard work. The feedback you receive from your clients will let you know you've found the right niche focus.

Study your new niche customer carefully: Become an expert in the unique circumstances and challenges your new target audience is dealing with so you can be their best solution.

Don't limit yourself to a single niche: It's important to carefully define your niche, but you can have a secondary niche as well.

Make your niche client your marketing priority: When your phone rings with an opportunity that is not in your niche, don't be afraid to turn down the business. It shows your commitment to making your niche your priority. It's indicative of growth in your leadership mindset.

Niche marketing is cost-effective. The more focused you are on who your customers are, where they shop, how they live, how often they buy things, what their values are, and what their struggles are . . . the easier it is to sell to them. By knowing your customer, you can make your marketing dollars go a lot further, too.

Team FIX
DISRUPTIVE PRODUCT TRENDS

Pull your team together to discuss technology or service trends, using my list or add ones that you've looked up. Are they transforming products, services, or delivery systems in your niche or marketplace? If so, brainstorm possible responses.

- Home systems integrations
- Face and fingerprint ID
- Marketing and sales automation

- Wearable technology
- Artificial intelligence
- Internet of Things (IoT)
- Augmented or virtual reality
- "On demand" everything
- Voice control
- Machine learning

Products vs. Services

A product business is much more scalable because it's not limited by the available time of you or your team. But many small company owners wait too long to outsource their manufacturing or packaging or other fulfillment processes, thus unnecessarily limiting their growth potential. Be sure that you are constantly exploring more efficient ways to produce your products, to improve your quality, to scale quantities, and to expand your market.

Service businesses can be scaled if you are fierce about "productizing" them—turning the way you do things into a signature process (see Chapter 5: Processes). Give your priority process a name and a Trademark (TM) or Service Mark (SM) and it becomes intellectual property (IP) with value of its own that can be replicated and scaled. Licensing and franchising are two ways to scale service businesses.

Pricing

I can't overemphasize the importance of pricing products or services correctly. Yet, many business owners don't devote sufficient time and attention to their pricing formulas. Do you know all your underlying costs so you can derive a price that's profitable? Are you including a percentage of your overhead and general and administrative costs in your pricing? What about your packaging costs? You need to know how much profit margin is in every sale, and your accounts receivable turnover ratio can inform better pricing as well.

Should you have good pricing or great pricing? Our first instinct is to have great prices that will permit us to crush the competition, gain market share, and fuel fast growth. The usual problem is that great prices typically provide slim profit margins. Good pricing, however, over the long term, should create enough profitability to make your enterprise a business rather than a glorified hobby.

If your product is priced too high, it won't sell. If it's priced too low, you'll be swamped with orders and have such a small profit margin, it won't even be worth the effort. Finding the balance is the trick. The challenge is developing a pricing strategy that is simple in concept and execution. How you create your best pricing will depend on your cost structure, type of business, your sales objectives, competition, and marketing strategy. Don't be emotional about creating your pricing program. It is the only way you are going to be successful.

What Goes into Cost

Calculate the total cost of your product. This should include your hard costs (labor, materials/inventory, packaging, shipping). You should also include a percentage of your overhead expenses such as legal, accounting, marketing, and administrative costs.

At the same time, focus on cost controls. Work diligently to drive your costs down because it will let you make more money without raising your prices.

Once you have all your costs, then you need to determine your profit margin to calculate the final price. Depending on what you sell, the profit margin could be anywhere from 30% to 300%.

Your pricing should:

- Highlight the value you provide your customers
- Earn you a reasonable profit
- Be competitive

Let's look at several different types of businesses and their different approaches to pricing:

- Brick and mortar retail/wholesale enterprises which depend on inventory to sell, typically price the goods on arrival. The pricing can be manufacturer's suggested retail (with or without discounts) or a standard markup of 50% to 100% depending on the item. Commonly competitive items, like a gallon of milk for example, should be shopped to be sure your price is close to that in stores like yours.
- It is important to feature the occasional "loss leader," an item you sell at minimal markup, to stimulate traffic. The overall objective, however, is to have an inventory mix that will give you solid profit margins at the sharpest price points possible (considering your competitors' pricing), especially on high-turnover items.

There are some factors, however, that can allow you to build generous margins with minimal competitive penalties.

- For example, my local convenience store has a 15% to 20% premium on much of what they sell compared to similar items in the local supermarket. The candy, soda, dairy products, and other grocery items are limited in variety, and customers typically pay without complaint especially when the purchase must be made when the supermarket is closed or farther away.

You can also charge more if your service is unique. For example, you repair certain luxury cars, or you are in industrial air conditioning repair, or a doctor with a specialty practice, or a lawyer who deals only with tax litigation. Typically, the more specialized and unique the service, the more you can usually charge.

What should you be thinking about when you are considering your pricing strategy?

If competitive conditions are good for you, that is, you have few competitors and solid demand, don't be afraid to squeeze out a few additional profit dollars in your pricing. You can always lower them later if competition heats up.

There is no such thing as the perfect price. It's all about developing a price that your customers are willing to pay that also makes you a profit. Because remember, profit is how we keep score in business. Pricing affects every aspect of business because price is used to create sales projections, establish a break-even point, and calculate profit.

Use your competitor's price as a reference point. If your product is of a higher quality, and you can demonstrate more benefits, then you can probably justify a higher price point. That will depend on whether the extra benefits and higher quality are important to your customers.

If you're selling luxury items, like jewelry or cars or homes or handbags or shoes, you need to be able to attract a group of loyal customers with the desire and money to buy these things. Most consumers will have to restrict their choices to certain price ranges where quality and benefits likewise compete within a different range. For different groups of customers, "quality" and "benefits" have completely different meanings and points of reference.

The goal must be to stay competitive. If your product is a knockoff, then your price point will be less and your customer base will be different. It's all about the perception of value.

Perceived value is one of the most common factors business owners use to determine product pricing. Unfortunately, some small business owners perceive their value to be much greater than their would-be customers, which is a great way to go out of business. The main factor that adds value to a product is the brand behind it. Lots of stores sell mixers, but if you have a Kitchen Aid mixer, you have a top-of-the-line machine. Why is that? All mixers basically function the same.

It's all about the perception of value. The Kitchen Aid mixer has a higher perceived value.

Let me give you a quick business lesson:

$$Price = (Labor + Materials) \times profit\ margin$$

What that profit margin is will depend on your industry and who you're selling to. If you're selling wholesale, you might double what your labor and materials cost. If you're selling retail, it might be double what you'd charge wholesale.

Don't Compete on Price

There's often a pull to be the cheapest seller on the block. Resist the urge, the race to the bottom is a race no one wins. People will assume your products are of lower quality. Someone will always be able to offer similar products cheaper than you, so this is a no-win situation. People pay based on perceived value. If you are confident—and competent—and can point to great work you've done in the past, people absolutely will be willing to pay what you charge.

Handling Discounts

It's easier to charge more and come down in price than to start out low and then try to charge more. If your prices seem to be too high for your marketplace, test out different promotions and see what price point resonates with your audience. Psychologically, you may see better results simply offering a discount occasionally than to reduce your prices across the board.

Test your Price Point

Pay attention to people's response to your prices. If you don't want to cut your profit margin down, consider adding more value to what they get, such as a free product or discount on future purchases. You can add value to either products or services by bundling them. Mix online services with face-to-face coaching. Add books or workbooks to consulting or training services. Add quarterly or annual maintenance checkups to repair services like plumbing or air-conditioning. Always be on the lookout for extras you can offer.

EXPERT INTERVIEW

How to Own Your Niche as You Reinvent Your Business
*Candid interview with business expert and
author Stephanie Chandler*

How does a business owner redefine their niche?
I like to start by asking a series of questions about your ideal
clients:

- With what industries or demographics do you most enjoy
  working?
- With what specific industries or demographics would you
  like to work? For example, maybe you are passionate about
  health and wellness and you'd like to work with people in
  related professions.
- Once you've identified some potential niche audiences, next
  you need to evaluate the opportunities.
- Is this a niche that is growing, flat, or declining?
- What is the competitive landscape for this niche? Is there a
  lot of competition or is there room for you?
- Try conducting surveys with people from your niche audience
  to determine their needs and challenges to ascertain how
  you might be able to serve them.

**Why is defining your niche so critical to long-term growth
in a small business?**
When you narrow your focus, you can better connect with
potential clients. I've carved out a niche for myself by working
exclusively with nonfiction authors. I have a passion for nonfiction
and the people who write it, and so I decided early on that it
would be my niche focus for the long haul.

**What are the most common business challenges when you
don't niche?**
Trying to be all things to all people can hurt your business because
you miss the opportunity to stand out. I attended a business

networking event awhile back where there were several life coaches in the room. Each stood up and gave a brief introduction, but they all sounded like each other. Then, a woman introduced herself as "a life coach for baby boomers who want to lose weight." It helped her stand out in a big way. As a result, she was surrounded by potential clients asking for a card at the end of the meeting. Had she not chosen a niche, she would have missed all those potential clients that couldn't wait to talk to her.

Your book, *From Entrepreneur to Infopreneur*, had a major impact on my business model as SmallBizLady. Can you explain why niching is truly beneficial to professional service businesses?
Thank you! Having a niche is critical for service-based businesses, especially when you have a lot of competition. I recently met a financial advisor who specializes in working with divorced women. Now, if you were divorced, would you be more likely to hire another general financial advisor in a blue suit, or someone who has experience working with people in your exact situation?

Here are some other examples:

- A moving company that specializes in employee relocations
- An attorney who works with family-owned businesses
- A business consultant who works with restaurants
- A personal trainer who helps busy working moms
- A website designer who specializes in ecommerce websites

What are your three top strategies for evaluating a new niche market?

> **Determine if the market you want to target is growing, declining, or flat.** You may already know enough about your industry that you can answer this on your own, and if you can't, some Google searches can help you gather research.

Evaluate the opportunity. Start by investigating your competition. Do you have a lot of competitors? If so, how will you do things differently or better than them? (Hint: this is where your niche comes in!) You've got to find a way to stand out, and clearly defining your niche will make you different.

Ask yourself if you will enjoy working with this market. Just because we can do something, doesn't always mean that we should. Choose a market that you can enjoy working in for a long time to come.

What is your best advice for helping a business stay focused on their niche market?
Know your audience. Learn about their challenges, wants, and needs. Stay on top of industry trends by reading related news sources. Survey your audience to better understand them and get out and meet with them in person. Learning how to serve your audience is the key to creating explosive growth for your business!

About the Expert

Stephanie Chandler is the author of several books including *Own Your Niche: Hype-Free Internet Marketing Tactics to Establish Authority in Your Field and Promote Your Service-Based Business.* **Stephanie is also founder and CEO of NonfictionAuthorsAssociation.com, a vibrant educational community for experienced and aspiring writers.**

FIX YOUR PRODUCT

EMERSON'S URGENCIES: SEEK HELP IMMEDIATELY!

If your business has become irrelevant, you will need to seek help and take action immediately to reinvent your products and services.

- If you are in a threatening position with a supplier, get legal help.
- What other steps can you take to save your business?
- Who else is available to help?

Write down your ideas.

1.

2.

3.

Is your product or product line up-to-date? If not, make a list of steps you need to take to make your business relevant again.

Identify any other ideas from this chapter that you want to act on.

FIX YOUR BUSINESS ACTION STEPS

Complete this chart of action steps and add your own based on Chapter 8: Product. Add an action step and target completion date for each.

	COMPETITIVE ADVANTAGE	PRODUCT MIX	PRICING STRATEGY	OTHER
STEP/DATE				
STEP/DATE				
STEP/DATE				
STEP/DATE				
STEP/DATE				
STEP/DATE				

Identify any Product or Service actions that should be included in your Strategic Plan, Chapter 11:

1.

2.

3.

CHAPTER 9: PRESENCE
BUILDING YOUR BRAND ONLINE AND OFFLINE

Anyone can secure a consulting contract or sell a product, but very few business owners take the time to build a brand. Once you build a business brand, that will set you apart from others in the marketplace.

What is your small business brand? Every business should have a clearly defined brand identity. Your brand is what your customer thinks of when he hears your company or product name. The brand is also the visual image of your business and how your signature product is expressed. When we think about corporate iconic brands, Coca Cola, Starbucks, Apple, and Nike come to mind. Each of these companies has strong visual colors and logos, and their products are easily identifiable to customers. I've been known as SmallBizLady more than ten years. For years, more people knew my brand name than my real name, Melinda Emerson. All these years later, both names carry a lot of weight in the small business world, but it took time to build up that brand equity, and I had to refresh my own brand as part of the process.

Where are you now with your business brand? Do you have a consistent logo and color story? What about a slogan or brand promise? My brand positioning statement is "Ending Small Business Failure." When someone goes to your website there are three things they want to know: Who are you? What do you do? and What can you do for them? That's the same thing people want to know when they look at your social media profiles, too. Do you have a consistent headshot and/or logo and business description on all the places people can find you online?

Having worked through Chapters 7: Performance, and Chapter 8: Product, you should have a good idea of whether your brand is solid and continues to represent your business exactly as you intended, or if your business evolution requires a brand refresh.

The goal of branding is getting your target market to see you as the one that provides the best solution to their problem. This is not something that happens overnight. It takes time to win your customers' trust and a deep knowledge of their needs to communicate your value clearly. These days, content marketing is key to establishing your brand online. We'll discuss this more later in the chapter. Let's get back to offline branding. Do you need to refresh your brand? I'm going to walk you through how to reposition your brand in the marketplace.

First, why do you think you need a brand refresh? Your reasons might include declining sales, loss of a major customer, innovative competition, or on the positive side, a new product launch, new location, or new cool technology. Look at your current brand. Does your brand position allow you to reach and deliver benefits that meet the needs of your niche customer? Your brand positioning is how to separate yourself from competitors by creating marketing messages that highlight a host of items including price, quality, convenience, product features, and distribution.

Here's a three-step process to refresh your small business brand.

Step I. Define What the Brand Stands for Today

You need to know how your customers feel about your company and your brand. Go talk to your key customers. If you target consumers, get in front of them. Try sampling at grocery stores or the local farmers' market, do surveys online with incentives, or try focus groups to learn insights. This process will help you identify both unmet and met needs and provide you with a current measure of the value of your brand to your customers. Look at your brand positioning against the competition. Conduct a SWOT analysis on your brand, including key strengths (as in your brand equity), explore weaknesses (such as limited distribution), opportunities (new niches to pursue), and investigate threats (as in your competitors). It's also important to review how your brand has evolved. Have conversations with your team or kitchen cabinet of advisors about what the company brand stands for today and how your brand has grown.

Once you know the current state of your brand, next you need to review what you sell.

Step II: Review your Core Products and Services

The purpose of Step II is to review what you sell and define your new brand. You should also identify a few new benefits of working with your brand and how you will promote the brand. Use your knowledge of your current market positioning and its value to customers or consumers to figure out how you want customers to think and feel about your new brand. You should also review your market research, consumer insights, industry trends, and the current purchase patterns. This review should include the current product strategy and mix, and if you're a service business, review the total service offerings and programs you offer. During this phase, you should also look at your production capabilities and limitations, distribution strengths, top accounts, and key selling points, along with a review of all marketing and promotional materials, including your website.

Use spyfu.com on competitive websites to see what keywords they use and if they use any paid advertising. Have someone call for a sample proposal. Buy their products to see how they package and ship them, and then return the products to see how they provide customer service. Also, pay close attention to their service offerings, keys to success, and any challenges they face. The goal is to determine how far you could move your brand without alienating current customers. You also need to identify how to attract new customers and build a loyal following.

When it comes to developing your brand identity or giving your brand a refresh, there are two schools of thought. You can hire a firm to help you create your brand, or you can pull together your kitchen cabinet of advisors and few close friends willing to work for food and have a good old brainstorming session. I recommend hiring professionals, but that doesn't mean you shouldn't do internal brainstorming before you hire a graphic designer or a brand strategy firm. It's good to have some good ideas about what you like and don't like, what you want and don't want in your new branding.

Team FIX
Brand Building

You need your team and advisors to weigh in on what your brand stands for in the marketplace. Get your team together to answer these branding questions.

- What differentiates your brand from the competition?
- What is your company's unique selling proposition?
- What kind of brand equity do you have in the marketplace?
- Who is your current niche target customer?
- Develop a detailed customer/client profile.
- Why do customers purchase from you and how often?

Hiring Help for Your Branding Efforts

This chapter is full of marketing questions, issues, and advice. As you go through this chapter, note the places where you are going to want help. Before you decide how much help or which kind of help you want or need, look at your whole marketing package together rather than doing it in pieces. Then you can work from a single plan that will be the simplest and most cost-effective while also being the most professional solution for your brand presence. Let's talk about hiring vs. outsourcing for marketing help.

- **In-house Marketing.** If you are primarily or exclusively an online business, you should build your marketing capacity in-house, and rely on your team to let you know when they need short-term consulting for a special project or a new capacity.
- **Outsourced full-service firm.** If you want a professional presence but don't want to do it in-house, spend the time to find a full-service agency that specializes in small business services.
- **Freelance services.** If you know what you want and what you should pay, it's easier than ever to find great freelancers for a logo or a set of marketing pieces. Go to **www.Fix YourBusiness.com** for more resources on where to find great freelancers for your branding projects. You can really hit pay dirt for all kinds of graphic design and creative services and keep them working with you for a long time.

Special Cases: Pay the most attention to getting help for website design and Search Engine Optimization (SEO) services. In terms of web design, you want to hire a firm that knows how to turn your website into a cash register. They must understand lead generation, landing pages, and how to position calls to action that convert visitors into customers. But often three bad things can happen. One, you can pay way too much for your website; two, you end up with a pretty website that doesn't covert sales; and three, you can be left with a custom website that requires you to pay the web designer for every single change! Unless you have a highly specialized e-commerce website with hundreds of products in your niche, stick with the website platform that allows you to make changes yourself like a WordPress website.

The second special case is hiring help with SEO: If you are looking to hire an SEO firm, be prepared to pay a monthly retainer for at least four to six months before you start seeing results. Ask for references and case studies. Call their references and ask how often they interact with the SEO company. Ask the reference if the SEO company is achieving their goals. You also want to know what type of reporting they include in their services monthly. Bottom line, you need to know exactly what they are doing for you. If they refuse to provide full transparency, do not engage their services.

Once you have a historical and current story for your brand, have reviewed the competitive landscape and industry trends, it's time to package all that information like a study guide and bring in your brand strategist or graphic design firm to help you develop a new visual statement and brand promise for your business. You've done the heavy lifting, now you just need to get your vendor up to speed on your business so they can start developing concepts, designs, and messaging. Let your team help you pick a direction for your new look and feel. The new messaging and branding must be designed to retain existing customers and acquire new ones.

Step III. Validate the New Brand

Now that you and your vendor have developed your new brand and positioning statement, you need to test it and validate it with key customers and consumers. Go back to the folks you asked for feedback in the beginning, including the focus groups and key customers you surveyed to see what their reaction is to the new brand. Be sure to share a new logo, website, or product packaging so they can see the brand in action. Their feedback will help you refine your new brand. The goal of this step is to finalize your new branding and solidify your brand promise. Once everything is nailed down, create a "brand style manual" that provides a clear direction on the new brand, market positioning, logo, color story, fonts, slogan, stationery, business cards, etc., and how everything is to be used in marketing and promotional efforts. This will become the overarching strategy for all marketing programs going forward.

Online Marketing Starts with Your Website

Your business must have a presence online. When running a small business, your website is often your most important sales tool. It's the welcome mat into your business. In today's marketplace, it is all about mobile first. The first thing many people do when making a buying decision is search online. Your #1 focus should be to make sure that potential customers can find you online and that your website is helpful. You also need to make sure it shows up well on a mobile device. Here are several ways that can help you increase your online presence.

Update Your Website

When was the last time you gave your website a face-lift? Keeping your website updated and professional-looking will help you look tech savvy to your visitors. Your homepage copy should include clear information on how you can assist your target audience with their pain points. Use a contact form, but be sure your e-mail and phone number are posted. (People do not like to buy from websites that look like the owners are anonymous.) Just make sure all the links work. There's nothing worse than going to a page and getting an error message.

Register Multiple Domains

One great way that could drive traffic to your website is to register multiple domain names, and then redirect them to your main website. For example, let's say you are a bakery. You might register bobscakefactory.com as your main website and then you could register sweettreatcupcakery.com and bestbakeryintexas.com, too. Then you could redirect the traffic from these secondary domain names using 301 redirects to your main website bobscakefactory.com. Domain name redirection could boost web traffic and increase brand awareness.

Refresh Your Keywords

Depending on the industry, the keywords people use to search for your products and services online can change as often as every six to eight weeks. Try to stay on top of the keywords people are using to search for your offerings online. Select the top seven keywords you want to be known for and make sure you use them in strategic places on your website and in your content. A good use of keywords is in blog titles and product descriptions.

Build Your Content Marketing Strategy

To build a content marketing strategy you must use the HELP mantra: Help Others, Engage People, Listen Carefully, and Promote Yourself with Care. Before you do anything online, you need to identify your niche target customer for your online efforts. Employ a listening strategy to figure out where your target customer spends time online. Research the keywords and hashtags people use most to search for your industry, services, or products. Then develop your content strategy for how you will stand out in the marketplace.

Keeping your website constantly updated with helpful content is essential to boosting your brand online. One of the best sources of content ideas is having a list of pain points for your target customers and highlighting solutions with your content. Blogging is one way to demonstrate your expertise. But you must always write for your customer. The more aligned you are with what content your target audience needs and wants, the better your web copy will match those needs. Link internally to previous content. You should be linking from one piece of content on your blog to another if it's also relevant. This will keep people browsing your content longer, but the spider web effect also will increase your search engine results. Don't put pressure on yourself if you are not a writer. Consider outsourcing content development to a freelance writer or develop other types of content.

Visuals are big online. If you have a product or service that is visual, like a bakery, post photos of your finished products or a video of you making your signature dessert. You can produce quotes on artwork, pictures of customers using your products, or infographics. Think about other types of content too, such as podcast interviews, brief how-to videos, or product reviews. Live video is extremely effective to build an online audience, especially on Instagram, Facebook, and YouTube. I've seen brands such as Jimmy Beans Wool in Reno, Nevada, grow their business to nearly $10 million in revenue by creating YouTube videos featuring their employees knitting projects. Professional blogs are updated with content two to three times per week. Producing quality content is a great strategy to drive traffic to your website.

Tips for Leveraging Visual Content

Combining images and articles. While you can cut down on the amount of written content you create if you use visuals as content, you're not off the hook completely. There should always be a description. Combining images and articles can get better results. In fact, content with relevant images gets 94% more views than content without images. By joining the two together, you can pack a bigger punch through your content marketing.

Invest in custom graphics. Stock photos have their place, but they're not what will spur thousands of shares. Custom graphics, PowerPoint slides, and images with custom text for social promotion tend to get people's attention better. Find a designer who can make your images unique at an affordable price.

Mix up your content. By using articles, custom branded images, infographics, and video you'll reinforce your core content and expertise. You'll also appeal to a wider audience and maybe give yourself a little break from writing.

Becoming the Face of Your Brand

In simpler times, all we had to do was brand the business and market our products or services. The concept of personal branding wasn't known much until the age of social media. I know this because I got started with social media marketing in 2007 and used it to build my SmallBizLady brand which now reaches 3 million readers a week online. These days, not only do you have to define your company brand, but you may need to become the face of the brand to make your business more relatable.

Your personal brand can be an incredibly valuable business tool. People want to associate real people to the businesses and brands they love. When you allow customers in, they feel a stronger connection to your brand and you'll build that trust relationship much faster. Whether it's on your blog, in social media, in print interviews, or on video, you should strive to position yourself as an industry expert. Consider writing a book or hiring a publicist to help you book media interviews. And when you are in front of the media, look for opportunities to educate the audience. Media interviews can help you position your brand more prominently within your industry.

Leverage Social Media

Choose the top two or three social media platforms where your target customers are hanging out online. Claim your brand on all the major social platforms, but do not feel compelled to try to be on every social media site. Be strategic with your time online. Use social media to connect and share your blog content and other relevant content. Use a 4:1 ratio of promoting other people's content over your own. Remember that social media is about mutual interaction and engagement. No one wants to be sold to, so don't just promote your business, share other relevant content to help build a community of followers who view your business as a valuable resource.

Right now, people spend more time on Facebook than any other social media site, but Instagram is the fastest-growing social media site. It's particularly popular among mobile device users, because phones are not only used for browsing Instagram, but also for submitting photos and videos there. Some brands have been most successful by showing customers behind-the-scenes looks at their businesses. Professional photos are best. It may be worth your investment to hire a professional photographer who understands Instagram marketing to take this type of photo for you or your products. If you sell products, you also want to make use of click-to-buy apps, so that if someone sees something they like, they can buy instantly. Head over to FixYourBusiness.com for click-to-buy app resources.

Your Calls to Action (CTA)

In all that you do to market your brand known through your website, e-mail, social media, billboards, interviews, podcasts, trade show appearances, signs in the windows, etc., you must have clear "Calls to Action." In other words, you need to tell the customer what you want them to do when they see your message.

Here are a few different CTAs:

✓ Like my page.

✓ Leave us a Review.

✓ Try Now.

✓ Download Free Coupon.

✓ Buy One, Get One Free.

✓ Call 1-800-My-Store.

✓ Sign up here for new recipes each week.

When your brand becomes very well-known in your niche, the logo or look itself sends a message. But when your brand is new or lesser known, you must be specific of what action you want people to take when they encounter your message.

Team FIX
Building a Marketing Plan & Content Calendar

- Bring your team together to make a list of all the marketing channels you are currently using including business development, content: blogging/podcasts, etc., social media, paid advertising, broadcast media, retargeting, paid search, press releases, e-mail newsletters, voice search, flyers, coupon mailers, newspaper circulars—everything that you use.
- Decide what will be your product/service push each month for at least the next six months. Work with your graphics team and copy writers to develop any marketing collateral, e-mail copy, and social media graphics at least a month in advance. Leave plenty of time for content/graphics to be prepared and edited. Once approved, all content should be uploaded to a project management folder that everyone can access.

- Develop a theme for each month or each week if it's a campaign and create custom content and social media messages to align with it.
- Create a monthly marketing calendar to determine which messages go out when, on what channel, and at what frequency. Since marketing involves so many channels, you need everyone organized and saying the same thing.
- Assign people to be responsible for certain channels, with dates and times to share content.

Invest in SEO

Search Engine Optimization (SEO) can make a difference to your website in search results. SEO is the process boosting the visibility of your website in search engines via "organic" or earned search results. There are three general aspects to increasing website rankings using SEO: Technical, On-Site, and Off-Site. Technical is how efficiently your website is running. When a website takes a long time to load, has broken links, and is not optimized for mobile or has outdated technology, these are all things that must be addressed during SEO. On-Site refers to the content on your website. It is important that the information is relevant to the keywords you are targeting. Make sure you have proper tags, whether it's title tags, header tags, meta tags, or blog post tags; these increase traffic and boost engagement, too. Off-Site SEO affects the ability to build "trust" with search engines via social media sharing, content sharing, social bookmarks, and local citations; the best is when you get an inbound link from a major trusted website such as Huffington Post or NYTimes.com.

Know Your Numbers

You need to know how your online marketing efforts are producing results. Every month, track the following:

- Conversions
- Phone calls
- Link clicks
- Cost per Lead (CPL)
- Cost per Acquisition (CPA)
- Keyword rankings
- Website traffic by channel
- Bounce rate
- Average time on site

Check your sales to see if you can trace any conversions to offline or online marketing efforts with CTAs (such as phone calls, link clicks). Then calculate your cost per lead and your cost per acquisition. Check your website's Google Analytics monthly to determine where your best referral traffic comes from, your organic search results, and social media efforts. Examine your keyword rankings, bounce rate, and average time on site. Do people leave your site quickly after they arrive? If they bounce quickly, you need to know why. Often it can be traced back to a cluttered website, lack of specific calls to action, or a poor shopping cart experience. Your SEO firm should help you determine this. Take note of your most popular content and give your audience more of it. You should also review your social media engagement goals and media impressions. There are quite a few social media scheduling tools and platforms that provide extensive analytics; go to FixYourBusiness.com for resources.

Mobile Marketing Efforts

Mobile is quickly becoming the go-to channel to reach consumers. If you're not using mobile yet, you will soon be as there are a variety of ways to get your audience to click to your website from the device that has their attention throughout the day. The average smartphone users look at their phone 150 times a day. Here are few ways to add mobile marketing to your mix.

Mobile Ads

Mobile pay-per-click ads can help you connect with the millions of smartphone users who are searching on their phones for businesses—especially local ones. Beyond mobile video ads (which should be no more than 15-20 seconds), there's growing interest in Google shopping ads, which are pay-per-click ads that allow you to show up in Google search results even if your target is blocking ads. Facebook ads are now mobile friendly and can help you boost engagement on your Facebook page. With over two-thirds of Facebook traffic being mobile, there is a lot of opportunity to leverage mobile marketing. There are other mobile ad options to consider, like banner ads, retargeting, and display ads within app content and on mobile websites. The key is: go mobile with your ads, because that's where your audience is.

Mobile Video

People now spend twice as much time watching videos on their mobile devices as they do watching on non-mobile devices. For this reason alone, business owners should consider investing in mobile video content and mobile advertising.

Mobile SEO

This is far beyond having a responsive website. Mobile SEO is about how your mobile website focuses on core ranking, indexing, and leveraging mobile keywords. Keys to success are the following:

- Focus on relevancy, usefulness, and authority
- It must download quickly
- Create a mobile index
- Fix mobile-friendly errors
- Do mobile keyword research and content creation

Mobile Search

You may have optimized your website for desktop searches, but you'll need to make sure your website is mobile search-friendly, too. Because so many searches for local businesses happen on mobile devices with intent to buy, it's imperative that your mobile website content uses keywords to attract local customers. Consider long-tail keywords that include the neighborhood your business is located in.

Voice Search

Voice Search is becoming a relevant way to market local businesses. Rather than typing in "best cheesesteak in Philadelphia," a user might do a voice search with Amazon's Alexa, Apple's Siri, or Samsung's Bixby. "What's the best place to get a cheesesteak in Philly?" Knowing this, you can use these semantic search phrases in your SEO to better reach your mobile audience.

Mobile Gamification

Whether you want to boost use of your mobile app, or get people to redeem mobile coupons, or have users share your content on social media, mobile gamification can help. Imagine a marketing campaign where you enter anyone who opens your app every day for two weeks to qualify for a drawing for a vacation. Or giving a coupon to anyone who shares your content on Facebook. By requiring people to make tiny efforts, it can have a huge impact on your mobile marketing.

If you truly care about reaching your target audience, don't ignore mobile. Instead, choose one or more of these mobile marketing options and see how they could grow your business.

Beyond Digital

If you have a brick-and-mortar store or provide direct services at people's homes such as a plumber or tree service or are a professional medical office like a dentist or chiropractor, you may conduct a lot of your marketing via direct mail, coupon circulars, e-mail and text appointment follow-ups, and local newspapers; and on the high end, radio ads, cable ads, and local magazines. But no matter how people find out about your business, they'll still search for your business online to check for a website or Facebook page, and any bad reviews on sites like Yelp.com or Angie's List.

Fortunately, you can accomplish a great deal through your online presence. But you may very well have a local reputation or niche in which people are not online very often, if at all; I certainly have never googled my local pizza shop. But I have certainly done a search in my phone for pizza near me when I was traveling on business. You don't need to do all the things I have laid out in this chapter, but you won't reach anyone without a clear brand and a basic online presence.

EXPERT INTERVIEW

How to Build and Maintain a Successful Brand
Candid interview with marketing expert Jay Baer

You've been in business a long time. How have you maintained your personal and professional brand online?
Consistency. I've written one or more blog posts every week for nine years and recorded one or more podcasts every week for six years. Personal branding is based on perspiration, not inspiration!

Does old-school branding still work—business cards, brochures, direct mail, etc.?
Yes, if you do something that defies expectations. For nine years, my business card has been a metal bottle opener. People come up to me at conferences and say, "Jay, you gave me your card in 2010 and I still have it. It's in my golf bag." If you know exactly where my business card is amongst your possessions, my work is done! Same thing with direct mail. There's a new tactic where you send direct mail only to people who recently visited your website. Huge impact and very relevant. That kind of thing works because people don't expect it. But doing the exact thing that people expect is a waste of time and money.

If you are reinventing a business, how should you get started rebranding a small business?
Make the story bigger. Don't focus on what you do, focus on what problem you really solve, and for whom. This allows you to play a bigger role in customers' lives. For example, people don't need socks, they need their feet to be warmer.

A lot of businesses are struggling right now with managing their business website, especially with mobile marketing becoming such a "must have." What is your advice?

If your site doesn't work 100% well on mobile, it needs to be a major priority for you. Soon, a majority of website traffic will be mobile (it already is for many businesses). And perhaps more importantly, search engines are ranking websites based on mobile friendliness. It can be an expensive hassle to redo your site, but if you're ever going to do it, do it now and think mobile first.

There are so many social media options. What are the top things you suggest business owner do to promote their business using social media?
For small businesses in particular, do not try to be everywhere. You won't have time to create interesting content in every channel, so just pick a couple. Which ones? The ones you like personally. The truth is, if you don't love something, you aren't likely to be very good at it. If you like Instagram, commit to being good at that. The only one that's probably a must-do is Facebook, just because it's so much larger than the rest.

How has content strategy changed, and should every business be developing content?
Yes, every business should be using content marketing. The best way to get started is to figure out the 50 questions your customers ask you most and answer those questions in at least two different formats. For example, use the same content for a blog post and a video.

In your book, *Hug Your Haters*, you talked about the virtue of negative online reviews. Can you help us understand this?
People do not believe reviews when they are 100% positive. It's better psychologically for your customers to see a couple negatives here and there. Further, every customer complaint is the raw material you need to make your business better. The most important customers are the complainers, because they tell you how to improve. Great businesses want MORE negative feedback. Mediocre businesses try to suppress negativity from customers.

About the Expert:

Jay Baer is the founder of Convince & Convert, a strategy consultancy that works with the world's most interesting brands to double their digital success using content marketing, social media, and remarkable customer service. A *New York Times* best-selling author of five books, Jay is the host of the Social Pros podcast, and is an inductee into the Word of Mouth Marketing Hall of Fame. Learn more at www.convinceandconvert.com.

FIX YOUR PRESENCE

HOW ARE PEOPLE SEARCHING FOR YOU?
Keywords: Do you know your top 7 keywords or phrases (long-tail keywords) for your business? As you develop your online presence, keyword research will tell you how to compete for search engine attention. Use **Google Keyword Planner** to develop a list of your keywords here and circulate among your team.
1.
2.
3.
4.
5.
6.
7.

Make a list of the reasons why you need a brand refresh. Then organize the list in priority order.
1.
2.
3.
4.
5.

What are the top marketing activities that currently drive leads into your business, then add three more you want to start utilizing to promote your business.

Current Lead Generation
1.
2.
3.

New Lead Generation Ideas
1.
2.
3.

FIX YOUR BUSINESS ACTION STEPS

Take these steps and add your own based on Chapter 9: Presence.

1. Identify the top 3 action steps that you need to take on your business presence. Decide how you will get them done (in-house, freelance, hire a firm, etc.) and the date by which you will take action. Add cost estimates as you get them.

Action Step   How to Do It   Start Date   Cost Est.

2. Determine what is the primary method(s) by which you will build the marketing functions of your business and mark them for inclusion in your Strategic Plan (Chapter 11).

3. Other

CHAPTER 10:PROSPECTS
CREATING YOUR SALES SYSTEM

In the last chapter, I talked about how to make your business visible to prospective customers in the marketplace—get them to visit your website or your store or to pick up the phone or answer an e-mail. In other words, get them to respond to a Call to Action.

Turning those prospects into customers moves from marketing to sales. The people responsible for these functions in your business should be working closely together in their strategy and implementation of tactics. They need to understand your target customer in the same way and share the same feedback about what works and what doesn't.

Many businesses allow marketing and sales to become warring silos as they grow, and I'll warn you now that's a path to destruction. So, start early to make sure you never allow that attitude to develop in your business.

Who Sells?

Even after several years, it's common for you to be the chief salesperson for your company. After all, you're probably the one who knows the most and cares the most about it, talks the most passionately, and gets out and around to the most prospects, especially in a B2B company. But long term, your growth depends on having other people selling for you.

Quick FIX
EVERYBODY SELLS

Every member of your team should be able to state clearly her or his specific role in sales. Ask them! Here are a few examples:

Bookkeeper: Sends invoices and collects the revenue for the company and tracks profits.

Customer Service Rep: Delivers services at a high level that leads to new sales opportunities and referral business.

Blogger: Creates content that helps to explain your expertise and value proposition.

Packer/Shipper: Demonstrates your company's pride in carefully packing shipments and providing on-time delivery, confirming their good decision to buy, and preparing for more sales.

Sales are the lifeblood of your business. Not only that: when you increase sales, that is what can take you to the next level. But if you're putting too much of your time into other areas of your business, you can't measure or even strategize on how to improve sales. Let's look at how to develop a sales strategy to grow your business. Of course, sales will become a part of your overall business Strategic Plan which we'll take up in Chapter 11.

Start with a Baseline

To grow your sales, it's important to measure that growth. You must know where you are right now. Dig into your accounting software or sales data to answer the following questions:

- How many customers have you averaged each month over the past year?
- What dollar amount is your average sale?
- Has there been any growth or shrinkage in your numbers over the past year?

Answering these questions gets you a baseline you can use to measure future results and improve from where they are right now.

If you can't get a simple, quick answer to those questions, go back to Chapter 4: Profit, or Chapter 6: Productivity to see the decisions you made about accounting and CRM software. Your bookkeeper should be able to produce those numbers, or your head of sales, if that's not you. You should also be able to produce those numbers from your Customer Relationship Management software. Make that happen promptly if it's not already there for you.

Decide What You Want to Achieve

Once you have a baseline, decide how much you want to grow it, and over what period of time. Pinpoint exactly how much money you intend to make. Then determine your strategy for hitting that dollar amount. For example, you might want to increase sales of all your products by a certain dollar amount. Or you might want to increase sales by X% for certain products or services. Maybe you want to introduce a new product, or increase pricing, or reduce the cost of goods sold on certain products. Your strategy should include the ways in which your marketing strategy will generate more leads, how your team will qualify those leads, and what messaging the sales team will bring to them.

Determine Your Sales Goals

Break up your annual goals into smaller ones. If your goal is **to increase sales by 30% by the end of 12 months,** break that down into quarterly or monthly goals. It might look like:

Goal: Sell $50,000 of our new candle line of products
How does this break down?
Office must sell $2,500 per week of new candle line
Get every salesperson to boost his numbers by 15%
Increase profit margin on all products by 5%

Each of these is a goal in and of itself, and they all should contribute to that overall goal of increasing sales by 30%.

Create and Assign Tasks to Accomplish Sales Goals

Goals won't achieve themselves! You'll need to create a list of items that need to happen to make your goals a reality. You might be the person to own these tasks, or you might need to assign them to others on your team. The action items for your sales goal might be:

- Hire two more salespeople
- Increase prices by 5%
- Invest $20,000 in marketing (social media, Facebook ads, direct mail promotions)

For each item, make sure it has an owner and a deadline. Many tasks can be (and should be) completed long before you measure results for that goal, so put them on a calendar and make sure the owner knows she's responsible for it. For items that will take more time, meet with your team regularly to track their progress and remove any obstacles that are keeping the business from moving toward that goal.

Getting in the habit of setting sales goals—even if you don't accomplish them every time—keeps your sights set on the horizon. If you want to grow your business, you'll need to focus on what you *know* your business can generate and what you *want* it to generate. But defining your sales goals can be impossible without an organized sales process. Often, sales is the last process to be designed and implemented in a business.

Organizing Your Sales Process

Your Sales Process is a measurable and predictable series of steps that you expect your team to follow and document from building the pipeline through closing the sale and following that customer through customer service, re-selling, upselling, and continuing interactions.

Team FIX
THE BOOK CLUB

I have visited some awesome small businesses where the owner started a Book Club practice. The company purchased multiple copies of a book for the whole team to read, and they got together regularly to discuss a chapter or section. There are lots of ways to try this:

- Invite everyone but include only volunteers.
- Require everyone for the first effort (if you have a small team).
- You select the first book, or ask a team to select a book.
- Start with a customer service book or a sales book focused on customer-centric attitudes.
- Check out FixYourBusiness.com for specific help on how to conduct an employee book club.

Build the Pipeline: You must always be working on generating leads, and sometimes those leads are existing customers. You need to have a process for building a sales pipeline and tracking customer contacts. Set sales goals for a given week, month, or quarter. As you learn to understand your sales cycle, especially in a B2B environment or in a big-ticket consumer purchase such as a house, a car, or a recruiter service, you may need to nurture a relationship six to twelve months until a new budget cycle creates an opportunity, an existing vendor makes a mistake, or external market conditions change the circumstances. We call these trigger events.

Automate the Sales Process: There are many CRM software tools, such as Insightly, Zoho CRM, and Infusionsoft that make automating the sales process easy, as I discussed in Chapter 6: Productivity. Track ongoing sales activities and leads from your marketing channels including referrals, networking, upselling, cross-selling, direct mail, paid search, organic search, social media, trade shows, PR, and website promotions. You should track open rates on e-mails and newsletters, and test sales messages with your target customers. If you use automation to create a predictable sales process, you can guarantee sales will grow.

Sell, Sell, Sell: In order to make a sale, you must ask for the business. You must make an offer to a customer willing to buy to make a sale. You must build offers into your sales process. Cross-selling is the art of getting existing customers to spend a little more money with you. Amazon is the best I've seen at this. They always let you know what customers like you also purchased. And it doesn't take a whole lot to upsell. It could be something as simple as a "Buy one, get a second item half-off" deal.

Thank Customers: No one owes you business. Be sure to thank your customers for their business. Showing gratitude with a personal call or note of thanks can go a long way. Over-deliver if you can. Surprise a customer with an early delivery of their products. If you build a relationship and constantly add value to the relationship, you will have a customer for life.

Monitor and Revise Your Process

The best thing about having a specific process for your sales function, and leveraging technology to run that process, is that you can learn from it and continually improve it. If you don't really have a process, you never know why you closed this deal and lost that one. You're always only guessing.

But when your salespeople have a step-by-step method to follow, you will be gathering data about what works and what doesn't work. If you lose deals, at what step do you lose them? Is it during that second visit, when the sales rep is trying to ascertain the prospect's real needs, or is it later when you're making a proposal presentation, or even later when you're negotiating contract terms?

Looking at the whole process will help you notice where there is a weakness in your process. Do you have a rep who needs more training on a certain step? Having a process and filling it with data gives you the power to learn, teach, and grow! Building an integrated sales process is the best thing you can do to generate revenue and watch it grow.

How to Hire a Salesperson

If you decide it is time to hire a salesperson, set yourself up for success. First, make peace with the idea that selling is essential to your business and start thinking about what you want in a salesperson. As my friend and national sales expert, Jill Konrath, always says, "You've got to know what you want to achieve in selling, otherwise your salesperson will have no guidance, and it's a costly mistake." So that this doesn't happen to you, I want to lay out a few pointers for hiring.

Start by Getting Smart

Just like it's a good idea to have a basic understanding of accounting even if you hire an accountant, you should also be comfortable with all the things I've already discussed with you in the last chapter and this one. Know your target customer, have a marketing plan, and be clear on at least a starter sales process so you can guide a new salesperson.

Personal FIX
DEVELOP YOUR SALES CULTURE

Sales is the lifeblood of your business. Your role as a leader is to cultivate a culture of sales in your company. Everyone should know their roles in sales, and individual salespeople need to be armed with information to grow and thrive or else move on quickly. Don't make the mistake of distancing yourself from the sales. Here's what to do when you are heading up the sales team:

- **Have regular sales team meetings** (monthly, or more often when the team is new). Set sales goals. Get their ideas. Help them focus on the right targets; help them qualify and follow up with the right leads; teach them how to generate the appropriate new leads. Make sure they are following the process. Work with them to change the process if it isn't working.

- **Meet regularly one-on-one to review key performance metrics.** Make sure they have specific goals. What is your expectation: amount of revenue closed? Track profit on deals? Number of deals closed? Number of deals in their pipeline? Review business closed plus review their pipeline. If a pipeline is inadequate, ask for specifics on how they are spending their time. Coach them toward improvement.

- **Ride along.** Go with your salesperson to a pitch meeting with a prospect or join in on a conference call meeting. Observe their performance. Coach them before and after. Let them observe you or others in a similar circumstance. Make these observations routine.

- **Develop a proper compensation plan.** Get help with crafting this. You must incentivize the outcomes you want. Be generous and be vocal in your praise for great work. You'll be creating a culture of continuous improvement and high performance. It's fine to have high expectations, but you also need to provide high support.

Know What You're Looking for

Before you begin the hunt for a great salesperson, decide exactly what kind of sales assistance you need. Are you looking for a consultant who can spend a few hours selling your products or services each week, or someone to commit full-time to your organization? How will you pay them? Commission, salary, or combination? The better you define the role, your needs, and your compensation structure, the more likely you are to attract quality talent.

Check with Your Network

I recently hired a saleswoman who was referred to me by someone who was an expert sales trainer in my professional network. Because our relationship started outside of my seeking to hire someone, I had a better understanding of her personality than if she had been trying to impress me in an interview. If you don't know of anyone who might be a good fit in your sales role, ask your network. That includes online and offline contacts, as well as even friends or family. Explain what you're looking for and see if anyone can send you a good referral. My new salesperson is amazing because the person who knew us both thought we would work well together, and we do. She's killing the game in my business.

Be Candid

When you meet with a potential salesperson, be open and honest about your needs. I cannot stress how important it is to find the right fit for your business and goals, but you'll only find the right individual if you share where your company is currently (even if it's not doing so well) and where you want to take it. Then sit back and let him or her talk. You want to find someone who has confidence and ideas about how they can help you make more money. They should have experience doing that for past employers or clients, and if they've already got contacts in your industry, all the better.

You can conduct a trial run with your new salesperson if you'd like. Work together for 90 days to give them a chance to get to know how you run things and see if they can dig up a few new sales. If you like their work, extend the offer to a permanent one. It's hard to hire a great salesperson, but if you get the right person on your team, you'll be able to focus on growing your business even more rapidly.

Training and Coaching Salespeople

Every sales rep will apply their own personality and unique touch to their selling *process,* which is a major advantage. When you establish a consistent approach, you can more effectively train and develop your team to sell with it.

Your company only grows if the talents and productivity of your sales team members grow. A well-outlined selling process allows you to set goals, evaluate performance on stated criteria, and coach reps who need improvement in particular areas.

- **Get Analytical**
  Don't rely on hunches or what "feels" like the best way to sell. Use your CRM to get a more precise view of what products and communication methods work best with different customers. Teach your salespeople to use the tools and insist that they do so. The more precise

your team's understanding of the needs, preferences, and primary motives of a buyer, the greater their ability to communicate value. People buy a solution that solves their problem.

- **Take a Step-by-Step Approach**
  With the limited opportunities a small business has, I strongly encourage you to consider the first impression your company makes with potential customers. Your sales representatives are called that because they represent who you are, your brand promise, and what you would do if you were there in person.

As you work to develop the performance of a sales rep, focus on the areas of needed improvement. Monitor execution at each selling stage, including lead generation, appointment setting, closed contracts, and customer retention. Some sellers need to enhance efficiency in getting prospects to agree to a meeting. Others need training on post-sale service to improve customer retention. All of them benefit from coaching.

If you are not an accomplished coach, I urge you to find some coaching opportunities for your key salespeople as part of your investment in their professional development. Visit FixYourBusiness.com for sales training and coaching opportunities for your team.

A big part of transforming your small business marketing and sales processes is painting a clear picture of goals and expectations. Give your sales team a framework that drives consistency and easy performance evaluation. Take advantage of technology to leverage their knowledge and your own.

Build Alliances

You have unlimited opportunities today to forge alliances with other companies or what I would call "selling solutions" or platforms to help move your products. It's easier than ever before, especially if you are selling online. You can sell products through platforms like Amazon, eBay, Etsy, or directly through social media sites like Facebook and Instagram and many others. These can be "virtual" products too, like eBooks (Kindle), online courses (Zippy Courses, Kajabi, Udemy), or any kind of tangible products, or combinations of both. You can outsource all the sales operations and fulfillment services if you wish and spend all your time producing products and driving traffic to your various web platforms.

Affiliate Marketing

Many of the teaching, training, and coaching-type products create the opportunity for Affiliate Sales. You can engage other online sellers to market your products to their customers in exchange for an "affiliate fee," typically 30% to 50% (sometimes more) of your total price. Likewise, you can become an Affiliate of other sellers, adding their products to your list or participating in special marketing activities and receiving a comparable fee for every item sold to one of your customers (LinkShare, ClickBank).

Neighbors

In your geographic neighborhood or your digital neighborhood, consider co-marketing with related but noncompeting businesses. Caterers with wedding planners. Printers with high school yearbooks programs. Apartment rentals with university student services. Movers with real estate agencies. Restaurants with local hotels. All kinds of for-profit businesses can find mutually beneficial ways to partner with nonprofits, too. Get to know the nonprofit agencies whose work you want to support and that your target customers care about. Find out what they need and how you can help. There will always be creative ways that you can do good while doing well. It's also a building your brand opportunity and sending messages to your market that go beyond promoting your business.

EXPERT INTERVIEW

Managing the Sales Function in Your Small Business
*Candid interview with sales expert and
author Barbara Weaver Smith, PhD*

What are small business owners' biggest sales challenges?
I work only with B2B companies, so I'm going to focus on that. Small business owners' biggest sales challenges are developing a professional, process-driven approach to sales. You should try to make your sales as much of a system as manufacturing or shipping.

Should the business owner ever give up having a sales role in the business?
The smart owner will always have a sales role, but not always be a seller and definitely not always be the main seller. If you always do most of the selling, you really can't build value in your company. Too much depends on you always being involved and maybe rests on your personal charisma.

But you always need to understand your sales process and how it works. I've seen owners hire a sales team and turn sales over to them. Soon you don't understand their sales jargon, you can't track their numbers, you can't hold them accountable, you're not making money, but you're afraid of them. They always have an excuse, a reason. What will you do if they leave and take your customers and leads with them? Truth is, nothing bad will happen. But owners are afraid. You have to own your numbers and your sales process. Delegate sales, eventually delegate sales management, but never delegate sales strategy.

What top things do business owners need to understand before bringing on a salesperson?
When you hire a salesperson, you need to know exactly what you expect her to do. Will she develop her own leads or will marketing find them? Is she experienced at selling the kind of

products or services that you sell and in a similar environment? A person who currently sells home security systems by phone knows nothing about how to sell training courses to HR managers in the field. You need to have your compensation plan clearly determined and be sure it's both fair and generous. You want your salesperson to be energized to get up and out every morning to meet new customers for you!

What kind of training and onboarding can you provide? Formal sales training as well as product training, or is it just sink-or-swim? Will this be your first person or is there a team she can learn from? A new salesperson requires a great deal of support, coaching, and mentoring to be successful.

How can small business owners avoid the feast or famine sales pipeline issues?

You can avoid the feast or famine sales pipeline with good business planning. First, if you have a seasonal business, maybe you can only afford a seasonal sales staff. Or, develop alternative lines of business to fill different seasons. Be diligent with cash management so that you can spread revenue and expenses more evenly throughout the year, including your salesperson's earnings. Pay a monthly base salary, and compute commissions annually, but pay commissions in quarterly installments.

If your feast and famine is accidental or because the sales team slacks off when business is good, work hard on quarterly goals and, if necessary, monthly or bi-weekly goals. Go back to the basics of how many calls or meetings are they having, how well prepared are they, are they targeting the right people, how are they spending their time. Be sure you are not eating up their time with non-sales activities.

How should a business owner get started revamping their sales process?

To revamp your sales process, start by choosing your CRM. Test out the sales process that's embedded in that or tweak it to match what you're currently doing if you have a process. Then bring your sales team together with sticky notes on a white board to see what's missing or what steps are too many. Add what should happen at each step. Keep refining it until it works. Get some outside help if you need it—this is important to do right!

You wrote the book, *Whale Hunting*, which is all about landing whale corporate customers. Why is it so important that business owners understand this?
Believe it or not, small companies can do business with very large companies. But big companies behave very differently from your average customer, so you have to learn a whole new process of how to find the right ones for you, how to approach them, and how to do business with them. Learning to do that well will transform your company in a very positive way.

What is the best advice you have for a CEO looking to reinvent their business?
Make your business all about your customers. Put them in the middle of every decision. Then spend your time developing your processes and helping yourself and your team get more productive.

About the Expert

Dr. Barbara Weaver Smith is founder and CEO of The Whale Hunters®, co-author of *Whale Hunting: How to Land Big Sales and Transform Your Company*, based on the collaborative culture of the Inuit people who engaged their entire village to hunt whales, and author of *Whale Hunting with Global Accounts*. Barbara teaches small and midsize companies to make more money through a complete business development strategy for bigger deals with bigger customers.

FIX YOUR PROSPECTS

EMERSON'S URGENCIES: **SEEK HELP IMMEDIATELY!**
If you are paying one or more salespeople who are failing to perform, if you don't know why, but you are afraid to fire them (afraid they will take business with them or damage your reputation), you need professional help from a good sales consultant right away.
Connect with me or talk to your key advisers for a recommendation. What other steps can you take? 1. 2. 3.

1. What is the current state of your sales operation? What is your revenue goal for next year? For three years from now?
2. Are you moving in the right direction with your sales operation to grow your sales according to your plan? If not, what is the primary action you need to take?
3. Are you the only salesperson for your business? If so, how long do you intend for that to be the case?

FIX YOUR BUSINESS ACTION STEPS

Take these steps and add your own based on Chapter 10, PROSPECTS.

6. Do you have a CRM installation?
   a. Is it suitable to grow with your business?
   b. If not, when will you make that decision?

7. Once you have a suitable CRM, you can develop your sales process.
   a. Are you satisfied with your sales process steps?
   b. If not, when do you intend to develop your sales process?
   c. Do you need external help for that process?
   d. Identify the kind of help you will seek out and when you will work on that process.

8. Identify the key ways you want to improve your lead generation and sales process and include them in your Strategic Plan (Chapter 11).

CHAPTER 11: PLANNING
UPDATE YOUR STRATEGY

Wondering why your business revenue is going in the wrong direction? It all goes back to that foundation you first created for your company—or sometimes *didn't* create—and how solid it was from the start. Everything since then should be built on top of that foundation, that plan. Without a strong and clear business plan, your business may flounder, and you've probably made a lot of costly mistakes along the way, which I'm guessing is why you grabbed this book.

The following are some of the most common problems I've seen business owners have with regard to their business plan.

1. It's Nonexistent

Maybe you never slowed down enough to actually write a business plan in the early days. Perhaps that's because you didn't think you needed one, were overwhelmed at the idea of writing one, or didn't know where to begin.

How to Fix It: Better late than never. Start today with a fresh business plan, or better yet, use this opportunity to develop a workable Strategic Plan from where your company is, to where you want to take it now.

2. It's Ginormous (and Therefore Useless)

Back when I started in business 20 years ago, you were taught that business plans had to be a thick 40 pages plus manifesto. They needed to be exhaustive and leave no stone unturned. Fortunately, that rarely applies to small businesses now (even if you are seeking funding from investors). If your plan is so overwhelming that you never actually take it out to review it, what's the point of having it?

How to Fix It: Try a simpler plan. I'd like you to have a plan that's readable and comprehensible, 10 good pages. Ideally you'll share your plan with key advisers and key members of your leadership team. Bankers, lenders, and accountants may also have a look. Stick to the basics, and don't strive for length. Just get to the point.

3. You Never Look at It

Maybe you developed a fantastic business plan . . . five years ago, and never looked at it again. Likely a few things have changed since your original idea of your target customer. Your plan should be a living, working document that you review regularly (at least quarterly) and modify as needed.

How to Fix It: Blow the dust off that thing and read it. Probably the structure can stay the same, but if you've pivoted in your product offerings, or your target market has changed, those need to be reflected in the new business plan.

4. It's Not Actionable

Maybe you stuffed your plan with $10 words and filled it with fluff. You read it now and it makes you laugh at how naive you were. You have no clue about what to do next to grow your business.

How to Fix It: Amend that plan with action items. If you established a goal of becoming a $1 million company, set up steps for how and when you can make that a reality. These need to be achievable and measurable steps so that the next time you review your plan, you can actually see how far (or not) you've come toward achieving those goals.

Quick FIX
Business Plan vs. Strategic Plan

Business Plan	Strategic Plan
Overall Design of a New Business	Ongoing Strategy for a Continuing Business
Focused on Business Model & Viability	Focused on Growth & Strategy
Written for Investors	Written for Founder & Operating Team
Deep & Somewhat Theoretical	Short & Very Operational, Pragmatic
Focused on First Year	Focused on 3-5-Year Horizon

A Business Plan and a Strategic Plan are similar, but not identical, and they serve different purposes. The Business Plan is the comprehensive overview of a new business, before it is started, and typically looks at its viability over a one-year period. It is written for investors, even if the only investor is the founder. The Strategic Plan is the operating and growth strategy, typically looking ahead three to five years, and designed for internal as well as external stakeholders.

Having a manageable and updated Strategic Plan is what

keeps your business on track toward achieving those goals you've set for yourself. Keep it simple, keep it updated, and keep it nearby so you can refer to it regularly.

Now You Are Ready

What you're about to discover is that having worked through the chapters in *Fix Your Business,* the hardest part of your Strategic Planning process is done! You've carefully thought through 10 of the 12 Ps of Running a Successful Business and now you're organizing them into #11, a planning document. But you've been planning all along.

The material you need—the reminders of what you want to do—is all captured in the last two pages of each chapter (or in your online templates or audio notes, however you took notes for yourself).

Now I'm going to show you how to organize them into a Strategic Plan that will help you look three years ahead. The plan is designed like this:

- 3-year goals, reviewed annually
- 1-year goals, reviewed quarterly
- Monthly goals, reviewed weekly
- Weekly assignments—these become tasks, to-do lists, etc.

You keep your eyes on the quarter, moving them back and forth from month to year. Get your team focused on monthly sales goals, making sure that the days are producing a good week's work and that each week is meeting the monthly goal. Do a good team review at the end of each quarter. If you don't meet quarterly goals, you won't hit your year. So what are you going to do about it?

That's the value of a Strategic Plan, and I doubt you've ever used your original business plan that way. It's not at all about micro-managing. It's about clearly outlining the big buckets of work that you intend to do, in order to reach the increasing numbers of outrageously happy customers that you intend to serve, and to achieve the purpose and revenue and profits that you intend to produce.

Let's look at an example. Here's a list of Action Steps I asked you to prioritize in Chapter 4: Profit:

TOPIC	1	2	3	4
Business Plan			x	
Budget			x	
Taxes			x	
Bookkeeping		x		
Banking		x		
Cash Flow	x			
Spending		x		
Revenue			x	
Profit Margin		x		
Pricing			x	

The instructions were as follows:

1 = it needs immediate attention, highest priority, take action this week

2 = it needs a FIX within my 90-day plan, get started now

3 = it can wait, save it for my Strategic Plan in Chapter 11

4 = I have this under control; it doesn't need fixing

This chart represents one owner's possible responses, so we can see that you immediately addressed your issues with cash flow. And you've already got things underway, or maybe even finished, with Bookkeeping, Banking, Spending, and Profit Margin. The items you identified for the Strategic Plan are the Business Plan, the Budget, Taxes, Revenue, and Pricing.

For your Strategic Plan, I would identify two big strategic objectives in the Profit area:

1. Implement an accounting system

2. Review pricing strategy on all products

Determine Annual Budget will be a goal as part of the accounting system.

Annual Revenue will be a goal of the Annual Budget.

Pricing will be one of the objectives that will contribute to meeting the revenue goal on a monthly and quarterly basis.

As you can see, the new things to be accomplished are in bookkeeping and a pricing strategy. Once they are done, they will be implemented and function as normal. Budgeting will be part of the bookkeeping process and will be reviewed and updated annually. Revenue goals will be set annually and reviewed quarterly.

To take another example, look at the Fix Your Business Action Steps at the end of Chapter 6: Productivity. I set you to work in that chapter on quite a few activities to consider how you could improve your own productivity and that of your team by leveraging technology investments. I don't know how far you've come with that work; it depends on how far along you are already and how far you'd like to go. It also depends on the resources you have available to invest in technology at the moment.

Step #4 on that list says, "Build a plan into your Strategic Plan if you have long-term technology needs." That simply means whatever needs you have to grow your business in any key area, make it part of your overall strategy where you can determine its priority in relationship to other needs and opportunities and budget for it in relationship to anticipated revenue and other expenses.

So you may add a strategic objective, "Develop long-term technology plan" with a 6-month or even 1-year deadline if this is important but not urgent, or if it requires a lot of research that will take quite a bit of time. Or if you've already completed your research, the strategic objective could be, Implement Technology Plan, with Phase I being a Year One Goal and Phase II being a Year Two Goal, each of those phases being spelled out in objectives and also being funded in your budget plan.

Matching Revenue to Expenses

In your home budget, you either have to save up the money to buy things you need, or borrow money on a credit card perhaps to make the purchase and pay it back with interest. The same is true for your business. In both environments, it's a big mistake to borrow more than you can comfortably repay if that borrowing can not immediately be leveraged for significant revenue returns. It used to be in the US that the value of a college education in the employment market was so high that borrowing the cost of tuition and other expenses was well worth it. Today, millions of students are burdened with debt for college degrees that haven't yet led to the high-paying jobs they expected.

Quick FIX
PLANNING TERMS

Don't get frustrated worrying about the difference between a goal and an objective or a strategy. Just think about your plan in common sense terms:

"Here's what we are going to accomplish." – (Goal)
How many, how much, how often, how big, by when, how good

"Here's how we're going to get these things done."
– (Strategy)

> *What we'll do, who will do what, when will they do it* (Objective)
>
> "Here's how we'll know it's working." *Measurement/Key Performance Indicators* (KPI)

You need to be very savvy in your own Strategic Planning and budgeting process to avoid miscalculation on your investments. Don't get me wrong. You have to invest to grow. But investing without a good strategy and a sound budget is madness.

Goal Setting

I know what you're thinking: I am tired of not moving things forward enough in my business. I'm here to tell you that the reason this is happening is because you are not measuring yourself against business goals. Are you one of these people who says, "Why set goals if you never end up meeting them?" Or you know you should set goals, but you haven't quite gotten around to it (like backing up your data or keeping your antivirus software up to date). I encourage you to shift your thinking about goal setting. When you take the time to set goals and follow through on those, it is an investment that pays. Here are six ways to look realistically at your business and create meaningful business goals.

1. Analyze the Current Situation

Look at where you are right now and ask yourself: are you where you want to be? It is imperative that you are clear with yourself about your current circumstance regarding money in the bank, accounts payable, your sales pipeline, and your processes. Once you have established what the present looks like, only then can you plan for the big picture and set goals against it.

2. Create a Roadmap

Focus on long-term goals in a 3-year benchmark when you develop your goal road map. These stretch goals have a place in your overall goal setting, but it is essential to set some clear, attainable milestone goals in the short term. Just as an undergraduate sets a goal toward earning a bachelor's degree before applying to grad school, your road map should include goals you can achieve sooner rather than later that will help you accomplish those long-term goals. You may even find that creating yearly measurable goals helps you clarify your vision even further.

3. Break It Into Small Bites

Create short-term tasks to achieve your goals for the next year. Creating monthly and weekly sales goals will help you move the needle on your revenue goals. Need to increase sales? Set a goal for increasing cold calls, social posts, and direct outreach such as attending networking meetings. Need to get people to your website? Establish a content development system and start an editorial calendar. Need better subscription numbers? Work on developing a new free download for your website. Remember: you can't achieve your goals if you don't take steps toward making them happen.

Mini FIX
"S.M.A.R.T. GOALS"

In 1981, George T. Doran wrote "There's a S.M.A.R.T. way to write management's goals and objectives." And we've been using George's acronym, with a few modifications, ever since. Here's my favorite version. When you write a goal, make sure it uses this system:

• Specific	Increase revenue, not "Grow our business"

• Measurable	Increase revenue to $1.5 million
• Achievable	Increase revenue to $1.5 million by adding two sales reps to our team
• Realistic	And adding a second shift of production in 6 months
• Time-bound	Increase revenue to $1.5 million annual run rate by 18 months from now

4. Stay Focused

It's not enough to set goals. Now you must make substantial efforts to attain those goals. For example, if you are going to be developing content, set aside one day a week to do that. Be proactive and set deadlines for your milestones in order to achieve those goals. It's easy to get distracted or discouraged, so keep trying even if you miss a milestone. One of the best ways to stay focused is to avoid or eliminate distractions whenever possible.

5. Work Hard

This is a time when hard work will determine your outcome. So many entrepreneurs spend a lot of time working on their day-to-day activities and don't allocate enough time and resources to commit to achieving their strategic goals, and then they wonder why they failed to accomplish those goals. There is a direct correlation between the amount of energy you put toward a goal and its results. Set your biggest goals first, then the annual goals, then the monthly and weekly goals. Help your employees do the same and be sure they have the tools to do so. Once you organize your time this way, you will see a difference in your business.

Pre FIX
TEAM PREP FOR STRATEGIC PLANNING
SWOT ANALYSIS

I highly recommend that you invite key employees and advisers to help you develop your Strategic Plan and conduct an annual review. Some owners have developed a transparent company culture where Strategic Planning includes everyone, or at least outcomes and financial reporting are shared with everyone.

If you are not prepared for that, however, try engaging your whole team in the SWOT analysis, which is great prep work for doing your Strategic Plan. It will give you lots of ideas and get your leadership team in the mood, plus take the pulse of your whole team on the state of the company.

Strengths
What do we do best? Process? Product? Performance?

Weaknesses
Where could we make the most improvements?
Profits? Productivity? Presence?

Opportunities
What external things could we take advantage of?
Expansion? New Product? Marketing Tactics?

Threats
What's going on externally that can hurt us?
Competition? Economy? Technology?

P.S. You can also conduct a SWOT analysis on one of your competitors!

Your Exit Strategy

When you start a business, it's all about passion and excitement. You burn the candle at both ends. You put in the hard work of planning to make sure you set up your company for success. The last thing you want to think about is getting out of the business. But that's a mistake. If you don't have an exit strategy, you could create a new set of problems.

What Is an Exit Strategy?

A plan to leave is an end game for a business. It's the ultimate goal of being in business. But if you don't plan ahead, it could be something you will plan for in panic mode, which is never good. You might not want to think about selling or otherwise getting out of your business now, but maybe you'll feel differently in five years. Additionally, if your business doesn't flourish as much as you expected, a well-thought-out exit strategy could mitigate potential losses and prevent you from ending up in serious financial debt.

Types of Exit Strategies

If you're ready to pull up your personal stake in the business, you have numerous options.

- You could sell the business to another company, an individual, or a manager.
- If you start a business with someone else, one partner might want to leave, while the other wishes to stay.
- Alternatively, you might want to keep your business in the family and sell to a relative or a group of long-term employees.
- You could also position your company for acquisition by a large corporation.
- If you grow your business to $100 million and you think it could one day become a billion-dollar company, then

you could also take your company public on the New York Stock Exchange. That means preparing an IPO or initial public offering. It's a long and somewhat costly process, but going public gives you access to cash and elevates your brand to a new level.

Often if you don't create a plan for your business future, a good situation such as a purchase offer or the worst-case scenario, like closing the business, could cause havoc. If you lose your largest customer, you might need to liquidate or go bankrupt to save your personal assets. When you are forced to sell your company to pay off business debt, you may or may not have any profits left over to keep.

Why Do You Need an Exit Strategy?

Your business's goals and plans aren't etched in 100-year-old marble. You can have multiple strategies that lead you in different directions.

For instance, a strategy that helps you build clientele, boost cash flow, and build brand recognition could allow you to stay in business for the rest of your working life. Alternatively, you could use those advantages to sell your business for a hefty profit.

Without an exit strategy, you have no alternative other than staying with the business and succeeding. Since you don't have complete control over either of those outcomes, you need a plan in case you need to take another course of action.

A wise small business strategy requires you to prepare for *every potential situation*. What if a competitor suddenly garners 90% of the market share in your industry? What if you fall ill and can no longer handle running the business? Nobody wants to think about those possibilities, but I encourage you to do so. The best small business advice I can give is to give yourself as many potential paths to success as possible. After all, you are not living to work; you want your business to enable you to live your dream life.

Expert interview

How to Plan For Success for Your Business
*Candid interview with legendary business
planning expert Tim Berry*

**How often should a business owner think about the future
of their business?**

I strongly recommend taking an hour or two once a month
to review your plan, track progress toward milestones, look at
plan vs. actual results, and revise the plan as necessary. What
matters is the process, not just the plan. If you don't use the plan
as a regular management tool, you're missing the main benefit.

**When you are building a Strategic Plan for an existing
business, how far out should you plan: 1, 3, 5+ years?**

You need to be much more detailed for the next year than
the following two; and much less detailed for five years. I
recommend that every business plan include monthly sales,
spending, and cash flow for the next 12 months, but only
annually for years two and three. And every business owner
should think and plan for five years in the future, but in less
detail, with a more broad brush.

**You founded the technology company Palo Alto Software
more than 30 years ago, and over the years your business model
evolved. What was your planning process to accomplish that?**

We did exactly what I recommend for all business owners: once
a month we reviewed our plan, assumptions, milestones, metrics,
and, specifically, plan-vs.-actual results for sales, spending, and
milestones. Sometimes we'd realize we needed to revise our
plan because our assumptions had changed. Sometimes we
needed to revise the plan because we were too optimistic or
pessimistic. And sometimes we decided we needed to stick to
the plan because we weren't executing right. We revised our
plan every time our analysis indicated we needed to. Some of
our planning involved long-term change that took years. We set

the long-term product road map, and then eventually executed a month-to-month planning tool for business owners.

You also successfully transferred your company over to your children a few years ago. How did you build a plan to do that seamlessly?

When my kids were growing up they had to help with chores like putting sticky labels on plastic disks, because we needed that done and we had no problem having them know where our money came from. But it never occurred to us that they might work for the company after they grew up. It was a nerdy MBA-built business planning software company, and we just didn't think of it as a family-run business. But things changed as they grew up, got their educations, and became adults. One of our sons joined to help with programming. He left after a few years, but then one of our daughters got interested in the business, and eventually ran marketing. Then 10 years ago, when I wanted to focus more on writing, she took over as CEO. Honestly, it wasn't a matter of planning. When our daughter settled in with the company and liked it, we considered that good luck. My wife and I never pressured our kids about the company.

How can business owners set themselves up in business to live their best life?

Every business has hard times and every business owner has to not just do what they like, but also those other things that need doing. I don't want to overemphasize the living your dream, because you have to do the work too, not just dream. And keep your priorities straight while you do it. Build a business to make your life better. Don't sacrifice your life to make your business better. I'm grateful that my wife didn't let me obsess too much. She insisted I get home for family dinner, even if I worked for hours, at home, after dinner.

How can you engage your team to implement your Strategic Plan?

Be aware that at the beginning of a new planning process, some people resist planning because they think it's about getting hard commitments that can be used against them later. Avoid this problem like the plague. Be very sensitive to having your team very involved with the planning process from the beginning, and make sure it's collaborative, not punitive. Look for opportunities to show people that when not meeting milestones is caused by outside forces, or poor assumptions, they are not going to be held accountable for what isn't their fault. Start with a SWOT. I've never seen a group do a SWOT analysis together without them thinking about strategy as they do it.

What's your best advice for business owners who want to reinvent their business model?
Make sure you have a good fresh look at your market, and changes, and a good focused strategy plus realistic milestones along the way. Keep a good lean plan up-to-date, and pull it up once a month in a 1- to 2-hour meeting to review assumptions, results, and priorities. Revise your plan as often as you have to. Make your planning process a powerful tool that optimizes management. And then manage the business based on what you discover as you review and revise the plan. Don't ever accept that anything is a bad idea just because it always has been a bad idea in the past. Review your hidden assumptions thoroughly.

About the Expert:

Tim Berry is founder and chairman of Palo Alto Software, and founder of bplans.com. He is a regarded software author, blogger, and angel investor. He is also the author of *Lean Business Planning: Get What You Want From Your Business*. His website is www.timberry.com.

FIX YOUR BUSINESS Strategic Plan

You can use any of 100 planning templates to write down the items of your Strategic Plan. These pages will help you sort out your planning goals and key activities, by quarter. Your notes here will enable you to figure out your budget requirements, and vice versa. For additional support, find the planning template on FixYourBusiness.com and download to your computer. Consider the coaching and training resources I've prepared for you there as well.

To put together your Strategic Plan, start by copying your Purpose and Vision from Chapters 1 and 2. Then, use your answers from the FIX Page and ACTION STEPS Page at the end of Chapters 3–10. Select the most important Action Steps you have identified from your work in each of the P-words. I suggest you limit yourself to not more than three in each category; and don't feel that you need to have three in each. These are your top, most important strategies for the next three years.

Strategic Plan Worksheet for _____
Date _____ to _____

	Purpose							
	Vision							
	Eight Areas of Action							
Action Steps	People	Profit	Processes	Productivity	Performance	Products	Presence	Prospects

Draw a circle around any Action Step that qualifies as a goal. An action is something that you can put on someone's to-do list and get it done rather easily. A goal is more like a project:

- Requires multiple action steps
- May involve more than one person
- Probably requires resources—money or human resources that you don't have yet
- May require research or investigation
- Something you are not ready to do yet

Write down the goals in any of your Areas of Action. You may have Action Steps that can be combined into a goal. List each goal in the row indicated by the year in which you'd like to accomplish it.

You don't need a goal in each area, each year. And it's okay to have more than one goal in the same area, in the same year.

A Process goal may also show up in Productivity; just as Products and Presence goals can overlap. Use your judgment as you work these out. Make your goals fit the plan, not the reverse. This is simply a tool to help you organize your ideas and information.

GOALS	People	Profit	Processes	Productivity	Performance	Products	Presence	Prospects
Year 1								
Year 2								
Year 3								

Ideally, I recommend you work with somewhere between three and six goals for an upcoming year. That will keep you plenty busy! If you have more than that, probably you can combine one or two into a more comprehensive goal, or you should push one or two into the next year. If you finish them all early, you can pick up a new one in Q3 or Q4!

When you've decided on your goals, move to a quarterly outlook:

	Q1	Q2	Q3	Q4
GOAL 1 Write your SMART goal	List Key Activities, who is responsible, budget implication, due date	List Key Activities, who is responsible, budget implication, due date	List Key Activities, who is responsible, budget implication, due date	List Key Activities, who is responsible, budget implication, due date
GOAL 2 Write your SMART goal	List Key Activities, who is responsible, budget implication, due date	List Key Activities, who is responsible, budget implication, due date	List Key Activities, who is responsible, budget implication, due date	List Key Activities, who is responsible, budget implication, due date
GOAL 3 Write your SMART goal	List Key Activities, who is responsible, budget implication, due date	List Key Activities, who is responsible, budget implication, due date	List Key Activities, who is responsible, budget implication, due date	List Key Activities, who is responsible, budget implication, due date
Etc.				

Let your team break these down into quarterly and monthly guides and weekly/daily task lists.

CONGRATULATIONS!

You've completed your FIX YOUR BUSINESS Action Steps for Planning. In Chapter 12, we'll talk about how to use planning strategies as a regular part of your business to keep managing your growth and your health.

CHAPTER 12: PERSEVERANCE
BEING STRONG ENOUGH, LONG ENOUGH, TO WIN

So many entrepreneurs I meet think too small. They're concerned about paying today's bills and give little thought to where they'd like to take their business down the road. That's an obstacle to success, but one that can be overcome with a little planning and strategy. But the most important thing to making more money is to believe that you can. Now you've started!

You've worked your way through 11 of the "SmallBizLady's twelve Ps of Running a Successful Business." Let's take a moment to review:

- Preparation
- Purpose
- People
- Profit
- Processes
- Productivity
- Performance

- Product
- Presence
- Prospects
- Planning

And here we are at Perseverance, the determination to keep at it. Keep making it better, keep being purposeful about your business and your life.

But I want to challenge you now, with your Strategic Plan in hand, to keep thinking about where you want to go with your business, where you want to be eventually, who you want to be as a business owner. You've got your house in better order now, and you're better equipped for success, but in all honesty, we have been focused on a lot of small fixes and everyday details.

So, before I go, I want to take you through a few big picture scenarios and close with the cycle of business planning that can make it all possible for you. Are you with me?

Here are three big-picture ideas to consider: grow your business to seven figures, take on extra capital to grow fast, or expand globally. Let's take things big!

Grow Your Business to Seven Figures

How would you start?

Visualize What You Want to Achieve

Don't be afraid to unleash your imagination here. Would you like to run a $5 million company? Sell it in five years and then retire and travel the world? You can't hope to grow to any level of success if you don't first establish what your goals are.

Write these goals down and develop a vision board. No matter how pie-in-the-sky they seem at first, if you think it, it can happen. It's not your job to judge your desires, just to record them. Seeing these goals on paper or a poster will help you get the right mindset to start believing in those goals.

Figure Out How to Get There

You wouldn't leave for a major road trip without a map. It's the same as a business owner. You need a plan for how you'll get to the destination (those goals you set). It may be overwhelming right now to consider becoming a $5 million company, but if you break that goal down into smaller ones, you'll be able to achieve them.

You've probably discovered the action items you need to focus on through your work in this book. Continue to work on them and assign time frames. You can even list tasks to complete each quarter to lead you to your goal. Build this into your Strategic Plan.

Find One Thing You Do Really Well

This might be a superior product. Or your insanely fast delivery time. Whatever that characteristic that makes you different (and better) than the competition, own it. And use it in your marketing material. You want people to know what makes your company unique from the second they discover you.

Hire the Right People

Few solopreneurs can reach that seven-figure goal without a little help. And there's no shame in hiring people who are smarter than you! Find professionals who can complement your skill set with other qualities and hire help to fill in the gaps with those tasks you simply don't have the bandwidth to do yourself.

Follow the Processes You've Developed

Success doesn't happen when you keep doing the same thing over and over. It happens when you pay attention to what's working and do more of it and kill what's not working. Be constantly diligent to ensure that you're firing on all cylinders and moving closer to that seven-figure goal.

Now, if you are going to grow a seven-figure business, you may want to consider outside investments to make things happen more quickly. I will help you consider various ways to raise money, but first I want you to think about whether you want to do that.

Do You Want Outside Funding?

If you have a growing business and you think you need more money to invest, I want you to hold your horses for a moment and ask yourself, "Why?" You need to get three different answers before moving forward. If you think that funding is the best option, be careful! Outside funding brings its own crop of distractions.

Here are five things you need to know before pursuing investors for your small business.

1. You Won't Write the Deal

If this is your first business, then you don't have a financial track record, which puts you in a beggar's position. The investor you seek funding from has the power and may deploy an agreement that puts you at a disadvantage, either by valuing your company less than you think it should be valued at, or by charging you a higher cost of capital.

2. You'll Be Chasing the Funding Instead of Customers

At this stage of building a business, there are few things as important as your customers. Once you divert your interest from your clientele to pursue funding, you will distract yourself from building your business. Customers are the linchpin of a successful business. Ignore them at your own risk.

3. You Could Undervalue Your Company

When you seek money from outside sources, you must place a specific monetary value on your company based on its assets and intellectual property at that time. It is difficult to calculate the value of an emerging company.

4. You Might Partner with the Wrong People

Partnerships are like other relationships. When you partner with an investor in haste, you put your business at risk. The offer to fund your enterprise rarely comes without strings, so make sure you understand your finances better than you understand your spouse.

5. You Could Lose Control of Your Company

Once you've put your most devoted efforts into building your company and secured outside funding, you'll have to appoint a board of directors, but most likely your funder will have financial and board control. Investors like to work with executives they know. You, as a fresh entrepreneur, represent an unknown territory. Backers don't know how you'll react to success or difficulty and may want to remove you as the CEO.

Now that I've warned you, let's look at sources of funding. Sometimes an infusion of cash is exactly what you need to take advantage of an opportunity to grow, to acquire essential equipment, people, or technology, or to meet the demands of your market so that you can focus on the company's growth. As the market changes around you, it requires constant adaptation on your part. The status quo is never an option!

Venture Capitalists and Angel Investors

If your idea is so big that you know the only way to bring it to success is with the support of outside resources, then angel investors or venture capitalists might be the right fit for your company. However, remember these investors are looking for a good investment. They weigh talent first and ideas second, so make sure you understand how to position yourself for this level.

What's the Difference Between Angels and Venture Capitalists?

Angel investors and venture capitalists (VC) are very different types of investors. Angel investors are usually private individuals who have some money and are keen to use it to get a return, but they may want very little to do with the day-to-day running of your small business. They may fund businesses with lower growth rate projections and be more interested in firms that create value in the community in ways other than high profits.

Venture capitalists usually work as a collective firm rather than individuals. They have deeper pockets, but desire larger and faster returns. They usually will require a much larger stake of your business to entice them to collaborate with you and may even take over financial management of your business as active backers. However, both types of investors will become your partners and require a piece of equity in return.

The best ways to appeal to an angel or VC firm is with a solid pitch. The main thing to keep in mind is to have conclusive evidence that your company brings substantial value to the table. Here are seven tips to make sure that you've got what it takes to attract this level of investor.

Tip 1. Know your numbers

If you've ever watched Shark Tank and seen start-up founders who fumble when asked what their profit margin or sales numbers are, you have witnessed how not being savvy about business finances can ruin a company's chance of getting funded. It is essential that you know these details of your business:

- Profit margin
- Sales (in dollars) over past year
- Gross profit
- Expenses
- Balance sheet

Before your pitch, spend time reviewing these numbers so that when you're asked about them, you don't trip over the answers and can confidently give a response.

Tip 2. Solve a problem

Make sure that your business solves a problem for which your customers need a solution. You should be able to convey to an investor that you understand this problem, as well as how and why your company is the best solution for this problem. Also, be keenly aware of your competition. An investor won't be interested in your product if it's a copycat of what's already out there. You need a unique angle and proof that customers want to buy it.

Tip 3: Have a track record of success

If you're struggling to keep your business afloat, this is *not* the time to seek funding. If you've been in business a while and have done relatively well, this is the best position to be in to ask for money. In your pitch you'll want to demonstrate how an infusion of cash could help you expand into additional product lines, hire more staff, or beef up your marketing.

Tip 4. Have an amazing team

Investors want you to have a strong team; they don't invest in solopreneurs. Your team should complement one another's skills and have management experience. Venture capitalists want to know there's leadership in the business that can withstand whatever challenge comes along.

Tip 5. Practice your pitch

Your pitch must be persuasive, thoughtful, and concise. You must be able to convey confidently your business plan and how you will use the money you are requesting. There is an art to delivering a strong pitch, so practice, practice, practice.

Tip 6: Show you're willing to help yourself

Investors want to see that you're doing everything in your power to promote your business, grow your network, and increase sales. If you can show that, it might be enticing enough to spur an investor to want to be a part of that momentum.

Tip 7. Always have the big picture in mind

If you have your eye on the big picture, you are guaranteed to keep things in perspective. Taking on investors is hard, and at times you'll need to swallow your ego and take advice that you might not like, but keep this in mind: you get a boss when you take people's money. Be honest with yourself about your venture and its challenges, and be willing to grow.

It can take up to two years of pitching to secure funding, so you need to stay strong in this process. Investors want humble founders who know the industry, the competition, the technology, the business climate, and regulatory issues. If you can be that person, hopefully you'll find the right investor to help your business grow.

Expand Your Business Globally

Since the introduction of technology and selling on the Internet, the world is getting smaller. Your competition is global, but so is your opportunity. You may find a lot of competition here in the States. However, there are millions of customers around the world that might clamor for your products or services. The state of the US economy might not always be as stable as it is today. Expanding your business overseas is a proactive approach to protect your business from an economic downturn. Your opportunity is unlimited.

Mini FIX
Why Go Global
Determine What You Want to Accomplish

It's imperative that you know what you want in terms of growing your business internationally.

- Would you like to find a US-based broker who can open you up to new markets overseas?
- Are you looking for contacts in a particular industry or country to assist you?

> - Are you looking for a foreign manufacturer to lower your production cost?
> - Do you need to deepen your knowledge of doing business in a particular country?
>
> **Write down your global goals in your Strategic Plan.**

If you want to do business internationally, it can be tough getting started, but the upside can totally be worth it. You may lack the contacts you need to build global business relationships. It may be financially challenging to fly all over the globe to make those connections. What can you do to start selling overseas?

Find the Right Network

The connections you need might be in your own backyard. There are organizations in your community that cater to doing international business. Look to your chamber of commerce to see what alliances it's forging with cities and countries around the world. You might be able to participate in international trade missions to build contacts.

The US Commercial Service is another valuable resource to help you build your business internationally. Not only does this organization offer trade missions, but it also provides webinars on useful topics like getting a letter of credit for international trade or working with a specific sector in another country. Additionally, its International Buyer program serves as a sort of business matchmaker, and you can find great business opportunities by participating in one of these events.

Internet Resources

Export.gov, a site hosted by the US government, provides a wealth of information and offers training opportunities from webinars to trade fairs and seminars. Their Discover Global Markets Business Forum Series is your opportunity to meet commercial diplomats, hear experts speak, and learn about US export programs. As a member of the site, you will get access to trade leads and market research. And if you live near one of the offices, you can receive counseling services in-person.

Travel Is Essential

If you're serious about growing your business in other countries, it is time to travel. But be strategic: if you're planning a visit to a potential customer or manufacturing partner, see what networking events are in the area. Doing business in foreign countries often requires building personal relationships over dinner. Learn the culture of the different countries where you want to do business. Doing business in India and Asia is very different from business practices in Africa.

Start with One Market

Once you decide what you want to accomplish, focus on a particular market. In China, Chinese consumers like to see cartoon-like graphics and pictures of people using the products. Chinese consumers are very deal oriented, too, and are always looking for the best buy. You'll need dedicated customer service staff who know the language.

For business owners who are yearning and motivated to start selling in China online, Alibaba is the most popular option. Launching a virtual storefront on their Tmall product is like launching a brand new business. Here are some of the steps to consider before your international launch:

1) Plan at least six months before launching in China.

2) Find experts who can advise you on the Chinese market.

3) Leverage Alibaba to help with your tech set-up.

4) Invest in sponsored advertising, and offer special pricing to be featured on the Tmall site.

5) Bring on business partners to provide translation services, and dedicated staff to provide customer service.

Growing your business globally takes a precise plan. It will take laser focus to get your operations up and running smoothly as your bottom line increases. Building new business relationships can be scary. There may also be delays as you learn government policies and procedures. Do not get anxious. Use wisdom. Allow time. Forge ahead and persevere. The benefits for you overseas could really pay off!

Your Planning Cadence

How did you use my book? If you took a deep dive with three big areas of need, you still have seven major business areas to cover to have a comprehensive Strategic Plan. Decide now when you will be ready to tackle the rest of them.

If you worked through all the chapters, you should now have a complete plan. You're ready to keep up with your planning on a regular basis. You can review your Strategic Plan each quarter and adjust it as needed. Be sure to involve your kitchen cabinet or your senior team in helping to vet your biggest ideas. Keep the plan in front of your staff so they always know the big picture of what your business is all about and where you're going together. And review the details and accountability metrics regularly and predictably so there are no unpleasant surprises on their end or yours.

Make planning a way of life, and "fixing" your business will become "building" your business and "growing" your business!

Staying Ready

As I wind down this book, I just wish we could sit down face-to-face and chat over a cup of coffee. I want to hear all about how you are doing, what you have planned, what is working for you, and what you have left to do! I want to be sure you know that I have been where you are. Recently, I celebrated almost 20 years in business. All the mistakes I warn you about—believe me, I have made them myself. Firsthand! What I have learned, I have learned through hard work, patient customers, awesome mentors, a supportive family, and by the grace of God.

So, my final advice for you is to stay ready. That IS how you stay strong enough, long enough to win! Even when you get everything in order and you think it's all set, you must be vigilant about your market, industry trends, and staying on top of the ever-changing needs of your customers. Technology will continue to force change, so pay attention to what's going on in the business community and the economy.

Be a student of your business and be a participant in your local network. In business, there's no such thing as just staying the same, just being satisfied. If you are not growing, you are falling behind. Because the rest of the world is always changing around you.

Visit my website at FixYourBusiness.com and use the resources we've set up for you. Join me on my live #SmallBizChat on Twitter on Wednesday night from 8-9 p.m. ET, one of my Facebook Live QAs on Thursdays, or come join my private Fix Your Business Facebook group so that you can get direct access and advice from me. Don't forget to subscribe to my main website, succeedasyourownboss.com, to get tools and tips to grow your business as well. Watch the website for news of special events just for you, and please let me know how your business is growing!

EXPERT INTERVIEW

Persevering For The Long Haul In Your Business
Candid interview with serial entrepreneur and author Twyla Garrett

You've run businesses for nearly two decades, sold one, and now you're building a few more. What keeps you going and wanting to still build businesses?

I'm motivated by the excitement of forming a new business, hiring people, and the possibility of scaling. Coming from the inner-city of Cleveland, I do not take it lightly being a successful business owner, and I thrive on the fact that I can put people to work, especially those who are in need of a second chance. Some of my firms hire ex-offenders because they have talents, but people look down on them. Being in business is an opportunity to shape the community. I believe in fostering a partnership with our employees.

When a business owner faces a major setback such as losing a big client or key employee, where should they start to rebuild?

Every business will have setbacks; if you lose a key employee or a big client, the first thing you have to do is regroup. Bring your key leaders; your CFO, marketer, sales manager, etc., and figure out your next move. If you don't have any of these folks yet, sit with some peer partners or mentors and figure out a strategy to move forward. Diversify your portfolio of clients so that you're not relying on one particular customer too much. And make sure that your employees are cross-trained so you're not at the mercy of any one employee.

You are an accountant by background; how important are the numbers?

I am an accountant, but numbers tell the truth no matter what business you are in. Any business person worth their salt has to understand the numbers in their business. It actually helps you predict your future or your demise and it also helps you determine if your price point is too low or too high. I would recommend looking at financials probably once a week. If you're bootstrapping financially, then you really need a number cruncher or bookkeeper. If you do not know your earnings before taxes and interest, then you cannot determine the best tax strategy or where your business is going in the future. The numbers tell the true story of the business. If you cannot manage a budget or understand what your financials are telling you, hire someone to help.

As a single woman who is a millionaire, you sold your first business, but you never married or had children. How do you define success?
I have been blessed financially, but when you ask how do I define success, I have one word, LONELY. A lot of times you forgo many things in order to build a business. When you run a business and you have multiple employees, and several businesses running at the same time, those things act as my children. I didn't have a spouse or date a lot of times because my business took precedence, but I allowed them to take precedence. Don't get me wrong, I'm not moaning about not having kids or a husband, but what I do know is that there is something called balance, and it's hard to bring that balance when you are growing a thriving company. Success for me now is being able to recoup my balance that I didn't have before. I spend time with family, and do the things I enjoy like traveling, speaking, mentoring, and writing books. Currently, my dating life is good and I believe that one day, God's willing, He will bless me with a husband.

How do you put the right team around you to win?
You won't know if the right team is around you until you go through trials and tribulations. I have been blessed to have some great employees who have stuck with me for many years and through multiple businesses. You have to be willing to let them bring their advice to the table and LISTEN! Make sure

to hear their views, foster collaboration, and allow them to be the dominant voice in the room. You have to sit back and survey your team and see what they bring to the table. Mentor them and help them foster what they want to do in the future. I think it's important as a business owner to know the goals and ambitions of each one of your employees and do your best to help them achieve their goals, too. Sometimes your best team member is not necessarily on your payroll, they might be an outside strategic partner or vendor.

What is your best advice for business owners who are reinventing their business?
Rip apart your business annually. It's the best way to decipher whether or not you have something real to offer to the marketplace. Look at those pieces that don't fit—remove them and see what's left. Then look at what you are doing extremely well and see how you can make it better and market it to other clients. Pave a new way by defining short-term business goals and come up with a tactical plan to move forward with accountability and measurement to track your success.

About the Expert

Twyla Garrett is an extraordinary serial entrepreneur, speaker, and government contracting expert. Twyla started off her career in the federal government and opened her first book-keeping firm in 1996. In 2000, she founded IME, which she grew to $25 million and sold in 2016. Never one to retire, she currently owns a GMS (general construction firm) with offices in North Carolina and Texas, and runs IRG, an independent claims management firm. Her goal is always to inspire entrepreneurs. She is also the author of the motivational book, *My Mother's Words*. For more information, log on to www.hiregms.com.

FIX YOUR BUSINESS REFLECTION

Go back to your PREPARATION ACTION STEPS from the end of Chapter 1. Use them to review and complete this activity.

Which method did you choose to Fix Your Business?	• 90-Day Plan • Deep Dive
If you chose Deep Dive, what 3 Ps did you select?	1. 2. 3.
What is your level of confidence about those business issues now?	1. 2. 3.
Of the issues I presented on the opening page of this chapter, which were most problematic to you?	
How are you feeling about those issues now?	
Of Emerson's 12 Ps of a Successful Business, which ones worried you the most?	
How do you feel about them now?	
Which ones were you most excited to work on?	
How did that go? How excited are you about what you learned?	
What issues do you want to remember from this chapter to help you later in planning?	

Did you get those issues resolved? If any need more work, be sure to put them into your plan.	
What was the Start Date of your 90-day Plan?	
What was the End Date when you completed Chapter 12? Did you meet your goal? Close enough?	
Make a schedule for reviewing and updating your Strategic Plan.	Put your quarterly and annual review dates on your calendar—do that NOW.
What is your next goal for using this book?	1. Work on a new set of 3 Ps. 2. Work my plan and use the book as a reference. 3. Take a new 90-days in a year or so. 4. Do a deep dive on one or more Ps. 5. All of the above! 6. I've had enough Fixing for now!

Once you've completed your 90-day turnaround plan, e-mail support@melindaemerson.com, including your name, business names, e-mail, and phone number, and be sure to tell us how you feel and how your business is doing, and we'll e-mail you an official certificate of completion.

CPSIA information can be obtained
at www.ICGtesting.com
Printed in the USA
BVHW092209280219
541487BV00003B/6/P